BEGINNINGS

BEGINNINGS

Keys that Open the Gospels

MORNA D. HOOKER

The 1996 Diocese of British Columbia
John Albert Hall Lectures
at the
Centre for Studies in Religion and Society
in the University of Victoria

TRINITY PRESS
INTERNATIONAL
HARRISBURG, PENNSYLVANIA

Trinity Press International, P.O. Box 1321, Harrisburg, PA 17105

Trinity Press International is a division of The Morehouse Group.

First published 1997 by SCM Press Ltd.
9-17 St Albans Place, London NI 0NX

Library of Congress Cataloging-in-Publication Data

Hooker, Morna Dorothy
    Beginnings: keys that open the Gospels / Morna D. Hooker
      p. cm.
    "The 1996 Diocese of British Columbia John Albert Hall lectures at the Centre for studies in Religion and Society in the University of Victoria."
    Includes bibliographical references.
    ISBN 1-56338-231-8
1. Bible. N.T. Gospels—Criticism, interpretation, etc. 2. Bible. N.T. Mark I, 1-13—Criticism, interpretation, etc. 3. Bible. N.T. Matthew I-II—Criticism, interpretation, etc. 4. Bible. N.T. Luke I-II—Criticism, interpretation, etc. 5. Bible. N.T. John I, 1-18—Criticism, interpretation, etc. I. Title.
BS2555.2.H67 1998
226'.06-dc21
                        97-46381
                        CIP

Cover design by Rick Snizik

Typeset by Regent Typesetting, London

Printed in the United States of America

98 99 00 01 02 03   10 9 8 7 6 5 4 3 2 1

THE JOHN ALBERT HALL LECTURES

Churchman, chemist, pioneer, soldier, businessman and philanthropist, John Albert Hall (1869–1933) emigrated from Britain to Canada in the last decade of the nineteenth century and made his home in Victoria, British Columbia. He left a legacy to the Diocese of British Columbia to found a lectureship to stimulate harmony between the Christian religion and contemporary thought. Colonel Hall's generosity sustained the work of three successive Canon Lecturers: Michael Coleman, Hilary Butler and Thomas Bailey. It also helped found the Greater Victoria Lay School of Theology. Since 1995 it has been supporting the lectureship's partnership between the Diocese of British Columbia and the University of Victoria's Centre for Studies in Religion and Society.

The Centre was established in 1991 to foster the scholarly study of religion in relation to the sciences, ethics, social and economic development, and other aspects of culture. As Co-sponsor of the John Albert Hall Lecture Series it assists in the fulfilment of the terms of the trust.

John Albert Hall lecturers are outstanding Christian theologians who address themselves to the church, the university and the community during a two-week Fellowship in Victoria, Canada. Publication of these lectures allows a wider audience to benefit from both the lecture series and the work of the Centre.

'The end of all our exploring
Will be to arrive where we started'

(T.S. Eliot, *Four Quartets*, Little Gidding V)

Contents

Preface

These four lectures were delivered as the John Albert Hall Lectures in Victoria, BC, in September–October 1996. I am grateful to the Diocese of British Columbia and the Centre for Studies in Religion and Society at the University of Victoria for the invitation to deliver the lectures, and for their gracious hospitality while I was in Victoria.

It has seemed best to publish the lectures more or less in the form in which they were delivered, but I have added references and occasional notes, together with suggestions for further reading. Full bibliographical details are given in the footnotes for those books and articles not listed at the end. I am grateful to the Revd Dr Ivor H. Jones for his comments on the typescript.

I am also grateful to Faber and Faber Ltd for permission to include quotations from T.S. Eliot's *Four Quartets*.

M.D.H.

Introduction

The theme of these four lectures is the importance of beginnings, and in particular, the way in which beginnings can help the reader to make sense of what follows. We have probably all experienced the bewilderment that occurs when the author of a novel launches into a story without any indication of time or place or the identity of the characters, and expects us to build up a picture slowly, as we turn the pages. How much easier it is when the novel begins with clear information that helps us to orientate ourselves. Other books, too, are more 'user-friendly' when they begin by giving us clear information about their intention and content.

Sometimes the opening paragraph of a document refers briefly to the topics to be dealt with in what follows; this, for example, was how letters in the ancient world commonly began, and so it is no surprise to find the same thing happening in the introductory thanksgivings in Paul's letters.[1] In the ancient world, too, writers often used this opening paragraph to offer a kind of preface, explaining the scope and purpose of the book: this is what Luke does in the first four verses of his Gospel. Dramatists sometimes provide their readers with the background information necessary to understand the play; we find Shakespeare doing this, for example, in the prologue to *Henry V.* Sometimes authors offer guidance as to the particular way in which they feel the rest of the book should be read, and occasionally this information contains significant hints as to what the end of the story will be. In the case of the Gospels, we are provided with background information, guidance as to the way in which each evangelist expects us to read his book, and hints of the dénouement of the story.

Enter a library or bookshop today, and you will choose a book because you are attracted by its title and cover. Before you decide whether or not you want to borrow or buy it, you will probably read the publisher's blurb on the jacket, scan the contents page, and check the preface and introduction, in order to discover whether the book is what it seems. In the ancient world, it was necessary to provide all the information conveyed today by title, blurb, contents page, preface and introduction in the opening paragraphs. Our evangelists have given us this kind of information, and we do well to heed it.

A Dramatic Key: Mark 1.1–13

'The end is where we start from'

(T.S. Eliot, *Four Quartets*, Little Gidding V)

Most of the twenty-seven books that make up our New Testament are letters. We tend to call them by the fancy name of 'epistles', but the word means the same thing, and we have no difficulty in recognizing them as letters. They begin with the ancient equivalent of 'Dear Aunt Rosie', give us the name of the author, and end with a greeting. But the first four books are classified as 'Gospels'. What kind of book is that? We imagine we know, because we're used to these particular documents, but it is difficult to think of anything else that is remotely like them. They tell a story about Jesus, and they have often been treated as biographies of Jesus, but they are very strange biographies. What kind of biography begins when its subject is a grown man, as does Mark, without any attempt to tell us anything about his childhood? And what biography begins with a great slab of theology, as does John? No biographer is totally objective, as you can see any day by comparing different biographies of Winston Churchill or Richard III, so we shouldn't be totally surprised if these authors have an axe to grind. But why are their books called 'Gospels', a word that means 'good news'? Clearly the men who wrote these books were making no attempt to be objective: what they were writing was propaganda for the Christian faith. The authors are evangelists, and their purpose is to persuade their readers of the truth of 'the gospel'.

The first thing we need to remember is that these books were written to be heard, not read. We are so used to the written word that we find it difficult to imagine ourselves in a world where there were no newspapers or magazines, a world where everything that was written had to be written slowly by hand, not on a word-processor, and where any copies of books had to be made laboriously, copied word by word: a world in which men and women were accustomed to listening. In that world, books were rare things. Few individuals possessed them, and if a Christian community had a copy of a Gospel, it would certainly treasure it. Our Gospels were probably written, first of all, for particular Christian communities; later, copies would be made and passed to Christian groups in other cities. We have to imagine, then, a group of early Christians, gathered together for worship, listening eagerly as one of the Gospels is read. Now there are important differences between the impact that is made on us by something which we hear and something which we read. When we listen, we have to listen intently or we shall miss something or forget it; when we read, we can always go back and reread an obscure passage. Reading has made us lazy listeners: we're told that the attention span of an audience is now down to a few minutes. Nevertheless, there are certain ways of helping an audience to follow what is being read aloud. When we listen, we need short, crisp sentences, or we shall lose the sense of what is being said; we will notice words which are repeated frequently or which sound alike. A chorus in a poem gives it cohesion; a summary in prose will help us to absorb the information we have been given. When we read, we can cope with longer, more involved sentences; we will notice things like chapter headings, paragraphs and italic type used to emphasize important points, and we will be able to flick through the pages in order to see the shape of the argument. So it is that if I am preparing lectures, I find that I write them in quite a different style from the one I adopt when I write books. In lectures, for example, I use short sentences, whereas in books I use much longer ones.

So when we study the Gospels we must remember that though we can sit down at home and read them through on our own, poring over each word, that was not the way in which their first readers – or rather, audiences – heard them. They could not analyse them in the way that modern scholars love to analyse them, dividing them into sections and sub-sections. They gathered together as a Christian community and listened to 'the gospel', the good news, being read. In the same way, even before the first of these Gospels was written down, they had listened to the individual stories – perhaps not arranged as yet in any particular order – being told by members of the community who had heard them from other Christians before them.

Imagine, then, the members of one of these early Christian communities, sitting listening for the first time to the story as Mark told it. We will begin with Mark because, though scholars continue to argue about the question, his was almost certainly the first of the Gospels to be written down. Listening to Mark's vivid words, his hearers could easily imagine the scenes he described; they could imagine themselves present with the crowds listening to Jesus in Galilee and with the disciples following him on the way to Jerusalem; they could feel the power of Jesus' summons to discipleship, and make their own response. There may have been no actors on a stage in front of them, but they were in effect at a play-reading, listening to a drama being read. Moreover, it was a drama that called for audience participation.

The idea that Mark's Gospel functions as a drama is a fascinating one, for a closer analysis of the text shows interesting parallels with contemporary Greek drama. According to Aristotle, the basic pattern of a tragedy is as follows: the circumstances that give rise to the tragic situation are explained in the 'complication', in which the various events that lead inevitably to tragedy are set out; next comes a 'turning point' or 'reversal' in the story, which is often a moment of discovery or recognition, when the characters grasp something of the significance of what is taking place; from then on the drama unfolds itself in the 'dénouement' (lit. 'untying') or working out of the tragedy.[1] The opening scene of the tragedy is termed by Aristotle the 'prologue',[2] and in practice this often provides the audience with whatever information is necessary to understand the play.[3] The whole thing may be rounded off with an epilogue.

Now one of the intriguing things about Mark is that there is a very clear turning-point in the story, half way through the book, in the scene that takes place near Caesarea Philippi when Peter identifies Jesus as the

Messiah.[4] From that point onwards, the nature of the story changes dramatically. Up to this point, Mark has concentrated on the impact made by Jesus on the crowds in his authoritative teaching and miracles; on the response of the disciples and the hostility of the religious authorities. From here onwards, the focus is on Jesus' forthcoming suffering; there are few miracles, and his teaching is mostly directed to his close followers, and concerns the nature of discipleship. The moment of recognition at Caesarea Philippi introduces a new theme which dominates the second half of the Gospel: the inevitability of the cross. According to Aristotle, this section of the drama is often accompanied by irony, because the events unfolding on the stage are comprehended by the audience, but not by the participants. But how is it that the members of the audience comprehend what is going on? The answer is that they are privy to the meaning of the events that are taking place, having been given this information at the very beginning, in the prologue.[5]

You may very well wish to tell me at this point that, however interesting this may be, there is one important problem in relating any of this to Mark's Gospel: namely, that the Gospel is not a tragedy. True – but to human eyes it *seems* to be such, and to many of the participants in the story it remains such. It is only those who read the prologue and the conclusion of the story who know the truth of the story, and know that it is in truth what Mark calls it – 'the gospel about Jesus Christ, the Son of God'.

So was Mark deliberately setting out to write the story in this dramatic form? Did he know anything about Greek drama? The Eastern Mediterranean world (including

Palestine itself) is dotted with the remains of amphi-theatres, where plays would have been performed, so Mark could well have attended them and been influenced by them. Or did he perhaps simply write, instinctively, in this way? After all, Aristotle was analysing what already existed; dramatists had written their plays before he gave them the rules about how to do it! The theory of 'how to do something' is always a logical analysis of what people actually already do. Maybe Mark simply wrote in this way because it was the natural way to tell his story. But *was* it the most natural way? Was it natural to begin with what is, in a sense, the *end* of the story – the disclosure of who Jesus is? It is as though, in writing a detective story, he has provided us with the solution before he has even described the crime. Normally that might seem a foolish thing to do, but we have to remember that Mark's 'audience' probably already knew the various stories about Jesus that he retells. In these circumstances we can understand very well why he might begin by telling us the way in which he wants us to hear his story, and alerting us to the particular features he wants us to look out for. As the story unfolds, we should see the importance of clues whose significance we might otherwise miss.

If there is indeed any validity in this comparison of Mark with a drama, it will be obvious that the prologue is a very important part of the book, and contains informa-tion that is crucial to our understanding of the story. So let us turn our attention to the opening verses of the book. But which verses? Are there any that stand apart, and seem to belong to the prologue, rather than the story proper?

A Dramatic Key: Mark 1.1–13

To answer that question, we need to consider the kind of material that we expect to find in a prologue. The prologue would sometimes be delivered by one of the characters in the play,[6] who would then take part in the play; sometimes it was spoken by the chorus,[7] who would continue to comment on the action of subsequent scenes; at other times it was delivered by a god or goddess.[8] Sometimes the prologue would take the form of an opening scene which enabled the audience to comprehend what follows. There is an excellent example of this in another biblical book, Job, in which chapters 1–2 describe the afflictions that have befallen Job, and explain to the readers (but not to Job himself!) why he has been overtaken by so much suffering. Often, the information given would be a kind of resumé of 'the story so far'. In the days when there were no theatre programmes to provide the audience with the information that would help them to understand the play, it was necessary to explain who the characters about to appear on the stage were and to set the scene, with any necessary indication of time and place. Because the comments were made with the advantage of superior knowledge, the audience was often supplied with information unknown to the participants in the drama: relationships between the characters of which they themselves were unaware, events that had taken place in distant places, future happenings that were in no way expected by those involved in the drama, all these could be shared with the audience in the opening moments of the play. The onlookers thus had an advantage over those whose story was being retold: they understood the significance of what was taking place in a way that the characters did not. They were, as it were, being privileged to view events from a divine perspective.

If you consult the commentaries, you will find that there is disagreement about which verses belong to Mark's opening section. Some scholars suggest that it consists of the first fifteen verses of the Gospel.[9] They point to the fact that Mark's opening words are 'The beginning of the *gospel* of Jesus Christ', and that in v.15 Jesus comes into Galilee preaching the gospel of God. The two occurrences of the word 'gospel' form, they suggest, a kind of *inclusio*, marking these fifteen verses off from the rest of the narrative. Well, perhaps; but is it not just as likely that the two references to the gospel are meant to stand in parallel, marking the openings of two sections, rather than the beginning and ending of one? If so, then the story proper begins with the statement that Jesus came into Galilee proclaiming the gospel of God. If we concentrate on the *content* of the opening verses, rather than simply the structure, we shall, I think, see that vv.1–13 stand apart from the rest of the story: for the information we are given in these verses is, to say the least, unusual, and the events that are described are rather different from the account of the appearance of a prophet in Galilee in v.14. The latter event might not be an everyday occurrence, but is not totally extraordinary, whereas a voice from heaven and the appearance of Satan and angels certainly belong to the realm of the supernatural.

Aristotle, not surprisingly, describes the prologue of a play as 'the beginning', and maybe the words 'The beginning of the gospel of Jesus Christ' are intended to indicate that Mark is deliberately giving us a kind of prologue, which contains the information that he wishes to share with us before we start to listen to his story. Let us look, then, at the information he chooses to give us in his prologue – at the key with which he provides us, in order to enable us to understand the story that follows.

His introductory words, 'The beginning of the gospel of Jesus Christ, the Son of God', alert us to the significance of what he is going to tell us: it is 'gospel'. As far as we know, Mark was the first person to write the kind of work that we would now call 'a Gospel', so that it was his use of the word here that gave the name to this kind of book. To say at the time that he was writing 'a Gospel' would have been a meaningless statement, since there was then no recognized form of literature of that name. The word 'gospel' means literally 'good news', and in the Bible it came to be used of a very particular kind of good news. In the Septuagint (the Greek translation of the Old Testament) the verb 'to proclaim good news' was used to refer to the announcement of God's salvation. What Mark is setting out to tell us, then, is the good news of the story of God's salvation of his people; and this story is about Jesus Christ, or Jesus the Messiah, who is also the Son of God.

Now there is some doubt as to whether Mark himself wrote that last phrase, 'Son of God', at this point. The words are not there in some of our earliest and best manuscripts, so we'll leave them aside for the moment, since we shall find them turning up again a few lines further on. What Mark has certainly told us is that Jesus is the Messiah. In the twentieth century, that is hardly likely to get us excited! We treat the word 'Christ' almost as if it were a surname; Christianity is by definition a belief that

9

Beginnings: Keys that Open the Gospels

Jesus is the Christ or Messiah. Of course the gospel is about Jesus the Christ: it is because Jesus is the Christ or Messiah or, to give the word its meaning, the anointed one, that the story that follows is good news. Nevertheless, we already know something that the great majority of the characters in that story do not know and few of them even guess; and if we are to understand the plot we need to realize that we are already party to privileged information.

The first thing that Mark has to tell us concerning the beginning of the gospel about Jesus Christ is that it took place 'as it is written in Isaiah the prophet':

'Look, I am sending my messenger ahead of you,
to prepare your way.
A voice crying in the wilderness –
Prepare the way of the Lord,
Make his paths straight.'

If you want to understand this good news, then, you have to realize that it is the fulfilment of the words spoken by the great prophet Isaiah, centuries earlier.

Now there are three interesting things about this quotation. The first is that Mark does not normally quote from scripture; indeed, this is the only place in the whole book where, as story-teller, he does so. There are, to be sure, several quotations from the Old Testament scriptures to be found in the mouths of his characters; but nowhere else does he stand back and say 'This happened as it was written in scripture'. In this, as we shall see, he was very different from Matthew. So even this information, that may seem to us pretty down-to-earth, is unusual. It is part of the key to understanding the story, giving us an insight which is not shared by those taking part in it – an important clue to what is going on.

The second interesting thing about this quotation is that Mark gets his reference wrong; only part of the quotation comes from Isaiah, and the rest seems to be a mixture of phrases taken from the books of Exodus and Malachi.[10] The fact that he attributes his only scriptural reference to the wrong author might suggest that Mark is a somewhat careless author! But we should not blame him; today it's a fairly easy thing for us to check a reference, for we can easily look up the quotation in a concordance, or even press a key on a computer, but Mark could use no such short-cuts. Searching through scrolls was a tedious business, and in fact he is unlikely even to have had the relevant scrolls in front of him as he wrote: he was probably working from memory. Moreover, Mark may well have been particularly excited by the fact that what the great prophet Isaiah had promised long ago had now happened, and so attributed the whole passage to him, for it is in the book of Isaiah, above all, that we find promises about God's future salvation of his people. The prophets had promised that a messenger would come to prepare the way of the Lord, who would bring salvation to Israel. The scene Mark is about to describe is the fulfilment of scripture: after years of hoping and waiting, the promises were at last being fulfilled.

And the third interesting thing is that the quotation which introduces the Gospel is only indirectly about Jesus; it is in fact about the messenger who prepares the way. The scriptures are already being fulfilled, even before Jesus himself arrives on the scene, but because they are fulfilled, we know that the person who follows the messenger will be the Lord.

The evangelist leaves the stage, and on walks John the Baptist. The scene is set in the wilderness, where John preaches a baptism of repentance. Notice how strangely Mark expresses this idea. We might have expected him to say that John appeared in the wilderness, baptizing men and women with a baptism of repentance; instead he says that John appeared in the wilderness *proclaiming* a baptism of repentance. If Mark emphasizes the fact that John was preaching, that is for a good reason, for Isaiah spoke about a voice crying in the wilderness, and now John appears, crying in the wilderness. The prophecy is fulfilled, and we know that John is the promised messenger. Even the details about what John was wearing and what he ate confirm his identity: the fact that he was dressed in camel's hair and wore a leather belt round his waist did not mean that he was a first-century drop-out; that was the way prophets dressed, so the moment we see John come on to the stage, we recognize him as a prophet. More particularly, if we know our Old Testament, we recognize that he is dressed exactly as the prophet Elijah was dressed in II Kings 1.8. As for his food, the fact that he ate locusts and wild honey tells us straight away that this is someone who is living in the wilderness. Later in the Gospel, Jesus tells three of his disciples that John is in fact the prophet Elijah, who was expected to return before the Day of the Lord.[11] The information is given to them privately but we, the audience, have been privy to it from the very beginning.

12

A Dramatic Key: Mark 1.1–13

If John is the messenger, then his task is, as Isaiah said, to prepare the way of the Lord. So he preaches a baptism of repentance, calling on men and women to turn around and to be ready for his coming. Mark depicts John's mission as a huge success: he tells us that the *whole* district of Judaea flocked to him, together with *everyone* from Jerusalem, and that they were all baptized in the Jordan, confessing their sins. If these words are taken literally, then the villages and cities emptied; it would seem that Mark is indulging in a little dramatic licence. But why? The point that he is trying to make is that the messenger has done his job; he has preached repentance, and so prepared the way for the Lord.

Mark's account of what John said is brief and to the point. Matthew and Luke have considerably more to tell us about John's preaching, but Mark's only interest in John is in his role as a messenger. Notice how his summary of John's teaching concentrates our attention on the one who is following him. Three times John is said to have emphasized how much greater than himself this coming one is. First, he declares, 'After me comes one who is stronger than I'. Now you and I, I suspect, would expect him to say 'greater'; so why 'stronger'? Later on in the drama, we find Jesus repeatedly exercising power, in particular power over demons. In chapter 3, we hear him speaking in parables, and describing Satan as a strong man who is being robbed by someone stronger: it's clear that he means himself. In chapter 5, Mark tells the story of a demented man who is possessed by many demons and has the strength of a whole legion of men: Jesus is the only person who is able to tame him. You and I, who know that

John's words apply to Jesus, understand why, but the characters in the story are overcome with astonishment at what is taking place.

The coming one is also greater in rank than John: 'I am not worthy,' he says, 'to stoop down and unfasten his sandals.' The point could not have been more sharply made: taking off someone's shoes was the menial task performed by a slave, so degrading a task that no Jew would perform it for another, but John considers himself unworthy to do this service for his successor. Mark has already told us that the one whose way John is preparing is none other than the Lord, and if that is so, we understand his humility, for 'the Lord' is the name used in the Old Testament for God himself.

Thirdly, John contrasts his own role, baptizing with water, and that of his successor, who will baptize with Spirit. John's baptism is a preparatory one, a baptism of repentance, but the baptism of Jesus will be a baptism with the power of God – the power that both destroys and creates, that purges and renews. John's baptism is a dramatic action pointing forward to what Jesus is going to do, and it is no surprise that later in the Gospel Jesus links his own work to that of John. In 11.27–33, when he is questioned about the source of his authority, he throws the challenge back: 'Was John's authority from heaven or from men?' The implication is clear: if John's authority came from God, then clearly his own must derive from the same source, because what John did spelt out the significance of what he himself is doing.[12]

Everything Mark tells us about John, then, directs our attention towards the one who follows him. John is, in effect, nothing but a human signpost, standing by the River Jordan and pointing offstage to someone else. So when, in v.9, Jesus arrives at the Jordan and is baptized, we know that this must be the one whom John has been talking about: and that means that he is the Lord, whose coming was foretold by Isaiah. What is Mark claiming? It can hardly be, as we shall see in a moment, that he is *identifying* God and Jesus. But certainly he is claiming that the advent of Jesus means the advent of God himself in salvation and judgment.

The strange thing is that John does not recognize him. Jesus comes to him for baptism, but he gives no hint in Mark's account of knowing who Jesus is. He was a signpost and nothing more. He does not know what *we* know. But if we have any doubt that Jesus is the one we have been expecting, assurance is provided from heaven. 'As Jesus came up out of the water, he saw the heavens break open, and the Spirit coming down on him like a dove. And a voice came from heaven: "You are my beloved Son, with you I am well pleased." '

In later scenes in Mark's drama all kinds of questions will be asked about who Jesus is, and all kinds of answers will be given. One thing is certain: a voice from heaven must have got the right answer! Here, at the very beginning, we are told who Jesus is. But what do the words mean? Centuries of Christian tradition have accustomed us to assuming that when Jesus is addressed as 'Son of God' it is a reference to his divinity. I doubt very much, however, whether Mark would have understood the word 'divinity'; certainly he never uses it. 'Divinity' is an abstract, philosophical term and not the sort of word that Mark uses or needs in telling his story. The word 'son' implies a relationship of some kind, but it is not necessarily a physical relationship; in the Old Testament both the nation Israel and the king were referred to as 'God's son', because they were in a special relationship to God. 'Son' can also be used to refer to a person who follows in someone else's footsteps; Paul, for example, describes Christians as 'sons of Abraham' because they share Abraham's faith. So when we are told that Jesus is God's Son, we know that he is like God, and that he shares God's character and authority, and perhaps we are being told also that he has taken on the role of the king, or even that of Israel. One thing that the idea of this special relationship would certainly have conveyed in the first century AD was the necessity for a son to be obedient to his father; and since Jesus is well-pleasing to God, we know that he is in fact obedient to him.

In Mark's account the voice is addressed to Jesus, and there is no indication that anyone else heard it. We *are* told that *Jesus* saw the heavens open and the Spirit of God descend on him. No one else, apparently, saw this; no one else knew: but those of us who watch as Mark tells his story see the Spirit descend and hear the voice speak. *We* know what no one in the story except Jesus knows, that whatever he does and says in the future will be done and said in the power and with the authority of God.

The Spirit of God has a very strange way of working, however, for in the next scene it is the Spirit who drives Jesus out into the wilderness, to be tested and tempted by Satan. We are told very little of what happened there: simply that Jesus was in the wilderness for forty days, being tempted by Satan. He was among the wild beasts, and angels looked after him. Matthew and Luke make a mini-drama out of this story alone. They tell us that Satan tempted Jesus three times; they tell us what Satan said to Jesus on each occasion, and what Jesus said in reply; and finally they round the story off by telling us that Satan gave up and went away. Mark does not tell us what the temptations were about, and stranger still, he does not even tell us what the outcome was! We assume that Jesus resisted the temptation, but Mark does not think it necessary to say so.

Now one of the temptations which *we* frequently fall into, in reading the Gospels, is to weave all the accounts together, into one big story, taking details from all the Gospels and piecing them together. In doing that, we miss the particular message of each evangelist. If we are to understand Mark's story, we need to forget the accounts of the temptations in Matthew and Luke, and concentrate our attention on Mark alone.

The first thing to notice is that the scene is set in the wilderness: 'the Spirit drove Jesus out into the wilderness'. Actually, the scene has not changed throughout this introductory section. Mark's opening quotation was about what was to happen in the wilderness; then John the Baptist appeared in the wilderness; and since Jesus came to John, his baptism must also have been in the wilderness. Anyone who has seen the Jordan will know that though the river flows through lush country, the wilderness is close on either side. But now the Spirit drives Jesus back into the wilderness proper. All these references to the wilderness would have had a particular meaning for

Mark's first hearers, for the wilderness held a special place in Jewish thinking. It was there that God had first revealed himself to his people, on Mount Sinai; and when God had delivered his people from Egypt at the Exodus, he had led them safely through the wilderness to the Promised Land. The wilderness was therefore associated with the ideas of God's self-revelation and deliverance; there was even a tendency to look back to the time spent there as a golden age. And so, naturally, the prophets looked forward to a new experience in the wilderness, when God would again reveal himself and save his people: that was what Isaiah had promised, and what Mark believes has happened. But the wilderness was also, of course, an arid place, and it was the place where Israel had been rebellious and had complained; as they journeyed through the wilderness, the people had even begun to think that their life of slavery in Egypt had been pleasanter! Later generations, looking back, said that the nation had been tempted, or tested, and had failed the test; that, it was said, was why the Israelites were made to wander in the wilderness for forty years, until they had learned to obey God and to listen to his voice.

We have said that in the ancient world a son would be expected to be obedient to his father. But one of the complaints of the prophets was that though God has treated Israel as his son, the nation had been constantly disobedient, not simply in the wilderness, but throughout history. God had called Israel to be his own special people, but they had refused to honour and obey him. And now perhaps we see the significance of that brief scene of the temptation in Mark's Gospel. For Jesus, too, has been called by God; he, too, has been acknowledged as God's Son; and now he, too, is tempted or tested in the wilderness. Not, it is true, for forty years, as was Israel, but for forty days: and maybe that number is meant to ring a bell in our minds and remind us of those forty years which Israel spent in the wilderness.

What, we want to know, were the temptations about? Matthew and Luke tried to answer that question, but Mark wasn't interested. What was the result of the temptation? Did Jesus resist? Surely Mark must be interested in that – but he doesn't bother to tell us! Maybe he thinks the answer is obvious: when Satan is confronted by someone in whom the Spirit of God is at work, then he has surely met his match. Certainly if we think ahead, to that scene in chapter 3 where Jesus describes his exorcisms as robbing the strong man Satan of his spoil, we shall see that he is claiming to have bound Satan, and to have done so in the power of the Holy Spirit. Mark seems to be thinking of this confrontation between Jesus and Satan not just as a temptation, but as a battle, a battle in which Jesus was victorious. Perhaps that is why he mentions the wild beasts, symbols of demonic power, and the angels who supported Jesus in the struggle.

We have come to the end of Mark's prologue, and in v.14 we begin the play proper. Jesus arrives in Galilee and proclaims the Kingdom of God. And no one knows who he is! No one shows any understanding of the things we know. Let us pause and think just what we have learned so far. We know that the story we are about to hear is the good news for which Israel has been waiting; we know that Jesus is the one whose coming was announced in the pages of the Old Testament, and who brings salvation to Israel; we know that he stands in a unique relationship to God and enjoys divine favour, and that the Spirit of God is at work in him; we know that, strengthened by God's Spirit, he has done battle with Satan; we know that he is God's Messiah or anointed one, God's Son, and the Lord. All that we have learned in thirteen short verses!

This information has been given to us in several different ways. First, we had Mark himself, informing us that he is telling us the good news about Jesus Christ, and quoting from the Old Testament: nowhere else in the whole Gospel does Mark comment on his story by quoting from the Old Testament. Then we heard John the Baptist preaching baptism and telling us all about the one who follows him; nowhere else in the Gospel does anyone give this sort of information. Then Jesus is baptized, sees the Spirit of God come down on him and hears a voice from heaven; now there is one other occasion in Mark's Gospel when a voice is heard speaking from heaven, namely at the transfiguration,[13] but voices from heaven are not exactly an everyday occurrence, and certainly we don't see the Spirit again. Indeed, one of the interesting things about these first three brief scenes, in which we see first John the Baptist, then the baptism of Jesus, and finally the temptation, is that the Spirit is mentioned in all three, for the Spirit is mentioned only rarely in the rest of the Gospel. As for that last scene, in which Jesus confronts Satan in the presence of angels and wild beasts, Satan is indeed mentioned elsewhere, but this is his only personal appearance on the stage, while the angels and wild beasts are 'extras' who certainly will not be required for future scenes.

A Dramatic Key: Mark 1.1–13

Things happen in the prologue that happen nowhere else; characters appear here who are not seen again, and truths are spelt out here that are not explained elsewhere. Only when we get to the *end* of Mark's story is Jesus openly proclaimed as the Messiah – in the accusation nailed to his cross; only then is he acknowledged as God's Son – by the centurion who executes him.

Jesus will be acknowledged as God's Son at the moment of his death: here, he is acknowledged as Son by the divine voice at the moment of baptism. Does Mark expect his readers to see a deeper significance in this parallel? Would they have known the teaching which Paul seemed to assume would be familiar to his readers in Rome – that in baptism Christian believers are baptized into Christ's death?[14] If so, then the reference to Jesus' baptism may well have been enough in itself to make them think forwards to his death. And in fact, later in the Gospel, we find Jesus speaking of his own suffering and death in terms of a 'baptism',[15] so that by the time Mark's readers had heard the story read two or three times, they would surely have made the connection. Mark has given us not only information about who Jesus is, but a hint of the dénouement of the story.

Imagine that you have arrived late for a performance of Mark's drama, or have begun to read his Gospel at 1.14; imagine that you know nothing of the significance of his story. Then you might well find yourself in the position of the characters in the drama that he is about to unfold: characters who hear the teaching of Jesus and are amazed by what they hear; who see Jesus performing miracles of healing, and are astonished by his authority; who watch his exorcisms, and wonder whether he is working by the power of God or of Satan; who ask themselves 'Who can this be?' and do not know the answer. But you and I know the answer; you and I have been privileged to learn the truth about Jesus at the very beginning of the story. Mark has given us the key which will enable us to understand the rest of the Gospel. And from time to time, as he tells his story, he will, as it were, nudge his audience in the ribs and say 'You see? You realize why this is happening?' Just as a Greek chorus explains the meaning of the events that take place in the course of a play, so he will make sure that we, at least, realize that the story he is unfolding is the good news about the Son of God, in whom God's Spirit is at work. Read his story for yourselves, and see how these opening verses are the key that opens the Gospel.

2

A Prophetic Key: Matthew 1–2

'What we call the beginning is often the end
And to make an end is to make a beginning'

(T.S. Eliot, *Four Quartets*, Little Gidding V)

If listening to Mark makes us imagine that we are in a theatre, then turning to Matthew may well make us feel that we are back in school. His Gospel, much longer than Mark's, reads far more like a carefully ordered textbook than like a play. Read through Mark and you have the feeling that you are being rushed from one event to another, like Alice being pulled along ever faster and faster by the Red Queen: one of Mark's favourite words is 'immediately', and he hardly seems to pause to draw breath between one scene and the next. But Matthew tells his story at a much slower pace, and he orders it carefully, in blocks of material: here a block of teaching, there a series of miracles. It's not surprising, then, that many people have thought that Matthew was a rabbi, a Jewish teacher. He has a message to get across, and he marshals his evidence carefully, to make sure that we grasp the point.

Yet in spite of the fact that Matthew has such a different

'feel' from Mark, he, too, is writing a 'Gospel'. His book contains much of the same material as Mark and tells many of the same stories; and the climax of his story, like Mark's, takes place in Jerusalem with the death and resurrection of Jesus. Indeed, if we write the two Gospels out in parallel columns, we shall discover that the similarities are so close that it seems either that Matthew has used Mark as the framework for his Gospel, or Mark has abbreviated Matthew. So how does it come about that the Gospels are so different?

Well, one of the major differences is that Matthew chooses to *begin* his story in a totally different way. It's only when he gets to chapter 3 that he takes up the story told by Mark, and even then he handles it rather differently; for the first two chapters, he goes his own way. In effect, he has chosen to write his own introduction – to provide us with *his* key to the gospel; and though much of the information he gives us in his introduction echoes the things that Mark told us, he chooses to give this information to us in his own way.

In fact many commentators argue that Matthew's introduction really extends to 4.11; on this view, the declaration from heaven that Jesus is God's Son brings to a climax the information that we were given in chapters 1 and 2.[1] It is true that 3.1–4.11 contains much 'privileged' information. The question we have to ask, however, is why it was that Matthew included the account of John's preaching and of Jesus' baptism and temptation in his Gospel. The answer is surely not 'because he *needed* them in his prologue', but 'because he thought they were important elements in the story told by Mark'. Coming as they do after chapters 1 and 2, the impact of these paragraphs is certainly not as great as in Mark. But whether Matthew meant us to see them as part of his introduction or not, it is appropriate for us to concentrate here on the material he has added.

Matthew was perhaps a teacher; but I sometimes wonder whether he was a very *good* teacher. Certainly it does not seem to me that his first twenty-three verses are the ideal way to capture people's attention! He begins by giving us Jesus' family tree: a logical enough beginning perhaps, but by the time one has listened to the statement that so-and-so begat so-and-so for the forty-second time, one may perhaps be forgiven if interest begins to flag. Matthew begins right back with Abraham, who was regarded as the father of the nation, and traces the line down through King David to Joseph, Mary's husband. The point of this is to show that Jesus could not have a better or more appropriate pedigree: he is a descendant of the patriarchs, and he is of the royal line. Matthew divides this long list neatly into three: from Abraham to David, he says, there were fourteen generations, and from David to the time of the deportation to captivity in Babylon there were fourteen generations, and from the deportation to Jesus, the Messiah, there were fourteen generations. Now this arrangement is not simply the result of Matthew's precise mind, sorting things into nice neat divisions. King David, founder of the royal line, was a very significant figure in the history of Israel, as significant in his way as Abraham; the descendants of David were kings of Israel, as he had been, right down to Jechoniah, who was taken to Babylon as a prisoner. That was another significant turning-point, and since then, the descendants of David have not ruled as king. But now, fourteen generations after the deportation, which was fourteen generations after David, who was fourteen generations after Abraham, we have Jesus. The number fourteen is significant, too: we may well assume that this is simply because fourteen equals twice seven, which is a sacred number. But more significant than this is the fact that the letters of the Hebrew alphabet could be used to represent numbers, so that each letter has a numerical significance, and that when we add up the total of the three letters that make up the name David in Hebrew – DWD – we get the number fourteen: David is the key figure in all this. So we have fourteen generations from Abraham to David; fourteen generations of Davidic kings; and a further fourteen generations until Jesus. Clearly Jesus must be the one who is destined to be David's successor on the throne of Israel.

Tracing family trees is by no means easy, as some of you may know; to go back forty-two generations is extraordinary. It's no surprise, then, to find that Matthew's list does not quite tally with the parallel list provided by Luke, nor with what we read in the Old Testament. Matthew seems to have lost one or two names from the list of kings. No matter: he has used the tradition to make his point.

To us, there is one major problem with this pedigree. Every line is exactly parallel – 'so-and-so begat so-and-so' – until we get to the last line, where we find a big hiccup: 'Jacob begat Joseph, the husband of Mary, who gave birth to Jesus, who is called the Christ'. In the story that follows, it will be quite clear that Matthew does *not* believe that

Joseph begat Jesus. So why has he gone to all this trouble to trace a family tree for someone who did not, in any physical sense, belong to the family? The answer is that Joseph took Mary as his wife, and that therefore he was Jesus' *legal* father. We may well think that the belief in Jesus' royal descent and in the virginal conception are inconsistent, but Matthew is clearly not bothered: *legal* descent is what matters, and that is sufficient for the point he is trying to make.

There is something else very intriguing about this list. The fact that Matthew traces the line through the men is hardly surprising, since he is tracing legal descent. He is uninterested in the women, with just five exceptions: he mentions Tamar, Rahab, Ruth, Bathsheba and Mary. Mary he could hardly miss out, but why the other four? If women were going to be included in the list, why not mention other well-known wives such as Sarah and Rebecca? Some names, of course, would have been forgotten – but not these. The editors of the recent 'Inclusive Version' of the New Testament[2] decided to put Matthew right on this one, and in the interests of equality they included the names of the wives of the men in his list, whenever these are known. This demonstrates how dangerous it is to tamper with translations, for in doing so these editors have completely missed Matthew's point. What we need to do is not complain, indignantly, because he has ignored almost all the women, but ask *why* he has chosen to mention these few. Is there anything that they have in common? Various answers have been given to that question, but the most likely explanation is that in every case there was something unusual about the union – something that might have given rise to scandal. Tamar disguised herself as a prostitute and seduced her father-in-law;[3] Rahab was a prostitute;[4] Bathsheba committed adultery with David.[5] The virtuous Ruth might seem at first sight to be the odd one out – yet even she made sexual advances to Boaz and risked scandal, in order to persuade him of his duty to marry her: moreover, the very fact that she was a foreigner would have seemed scandalous to some Jews.[6] And Mary, of course, is about to be found to be pregnant before her marriage to Joseph. Is this why these particular women are mentioned? Are these scandalous liaisons in the past a precedent, as it were, for what may appear to be the suspicious circumstances surrounding the birth of Jesus? If God was at work in the past, even when there was good ground for suspicion, and the messianic line was preserved through these women, is it surprising, Matthew seems to be saying, if questions have been raised about the birth of the Messiah himself? But *if* God was at work in the past, even in these strange circumstances, then we can be sure that he is at work in the birth of Jesus.

Matthew began his book with an introductory title. Translated literally, it runs 'The book of the origin of Jesus Christ, son of David, son of Abraham'. Some scholars regard it as a title for the whole book, but it seems more appropriate as a summary of the first seventeen verses, and the phrase 'the book of the origin' is used in Gen. 5.1 to introduce the list of Adam's descendants, down as far as Noah; in other words, the phrase means 'genealogy'. And that, of course, is what Matthew has given us; the title sums up the important points in that genealogy: he is tracing the legal line of Jesus, who is the Messiah, the son of David, the son of Abraham.

But that word 'origin' is also a significant one. In Greek, the word is *genesis*, and can mean both 'origin' and 'beginning'. It's the word that we use as a title for the first book of the Bible, which is both the beginning of the scriptures and the story of what happened at the beginning of time. Now Mark, too, you remember, began his Gospel with the words 'The beginning', though he was using a different Greek word, *archē*. Can it be that both evangelists, in their different ways, are trying to tell us that the beginning of the story of Jesus lies in the purpose of God? In tracing Jesus' line back to Abraham, Matthew is telling us that Jesus has been part of God's plan from the very beginning of the nation.

In 1.18 Matthew turns from genealogy to story. And we, his modern readers, move from a list of names that we have probably never bothered to read to the words which are familiar as the beginning of the Christmas story. 'The birth of Jesus the Messiah was like this . . .' That, at least, is how we usually translate the opening line of this section. In actual fact, the word that Matthew uses here is once again the word *genesis* – 'The *genesis* of Jesus the Messiah . . .' Some later scribes obviously thought there was a mistake, and wrote in another, very similar word, which has the more specific meaning of 'birth'. So was there some special reason why Matthew chose to use this particular word, *genesis*, which has a much wider meaning? Is he still thinking of the 'beginning' or 'origin' of Jesus?

The answer to that question is surely 'Yes', for if we

read through the next paragraph, vv.18–25, we shall see that it is *not* about the birth of Jesus, but about the fact that Mary was pregnant before her marriage to Joseph. Even before we come to the story of his birth, in chapter 2, we are told that his conception was the result of the work of the Holy Spirit. For the moment, then, we are clearly being told about Jesus' 'origin' or 'beginning', rather than his birth. Matthew holds together two ideas that seem to us to be contradictory: on the one hand, his descent (through Joseph) from the royal line; on the other, his conception through the Holy Spirit. And both tell us about Jesus' 'origin'.[7]

And because we are being told Jesus' credentials, everything is explained. As in the opening verses of Mark, we, the audience, understand the momentous character of what is going on: indeed, we know more than the characters in the story. Jesus, we are told once again, was the Messiah. Before his parents were married, Mary was found to be pregnant *by the Holy Spirit*; here is the apparently scandalous event that might have raised suspicions about Jesus' birth. Joseph, however, is now apprised of the truth in a dream by an angel. Throughout these first two chapters, angels regularly appear in dreams, and of course we understand that angels are messengers of God, and that we can rely on what they say. Joseph is assured that the creative power of the Holy Spirit is at work in Mary. They are to name the child 'Jesus', because he will save his people from their sins.

Names have meaning; today we rarely think about their meaning, except when agonizing over what to call the new baby. Among the Jews, the meaning of names had particular significance. The name 'Jesus' or 'Joshua' in its Hebrew form means 'God saves'. It was an appropriate name for Joshua, who led the Israelites into the Promised Land, and it is an appropriate name for Jesus the Messiah, but the name itself tells us nothing about *how* God saves, or *to* what or *from* what. It is not at all surprising to find Matthew explaining that Jesus is going to save his people from their sins, because that is one of the themes he brings out later in his Gospel. Here, at the very beginning, Matthew sees the name as significant, and explains the particular significance he sees in it.

Even more typical of Matthew is what comes next. 'All this,' he says, 'took place in order to fulfil what was spoken by the Lord through the prophet, saying . . .' This is a formula which Matthew is going to use repeatedly, especially in these first two chapters. Mark, you remember, gave us one introductory 'proof-text' at the very beginning of his opening paragraph, and then got on with his story. Matthew, by contrast, goes to town on the theme of the fulfilment of prophecy. He is going to make quite sure that we understand the way in which the scriptures are being fulfilled in what Jesus is and does and says.

The particular text that he sees fulfilled here is one of the most familiar passages in the Old Testament:

'Behold, a virgin shall conceive and bear a son,
and they shall name him "Emmanuel".'[8]

You may well feel that this text is not a very good one to back up what Matthew has told us. Joseph has been instructed to name the child 'Jesus', not 'Emmanuel'! At a literal level, the proof-text doesn't work very well: but as an overall judgment on what has taken place, it is right on the ball. The name 'Emmanuel', Matthew explains, means 'God with us'; the story he is about to tell us is the story of God at work, through Jesus, saving his people. The child who is about to be born *will* be known as 'Emmanuel', in the sense that in later days men and women will say that, through him, God was with them.

There is, however, another problem with this particular proof-text. Christians have long regarded it as a 'messianic prophecy', and supposed that Isaiah was looking forward to the birth of Jesus. In fact, scholars now believe that Isaiah was giving a message of hope to the people of his day,[9] and offering them a sign that God would save them. At the time, Jerusalem was being beseiged by enemy armies; a young woman is about to have a baby, says Isaiah, and it will be a boy, and as a sign of hope, she will give him the name *Emmanuel*: 'God is with us'. Before that child is weaned, the enemy armies will be destroyed, and Jerusalem will be saved. Isaiah's message, then, was not originally about something that would happen seven or eight centuries later, but was meant to encourage his contemporaries. When the Hebrew scriptures were translated into Greek, the Hebrew word for 'young woman' was translated by the Greek noun *parthenos*, which means 'a virgin'. By ignoring the original context, and treating the verse as a promise for the future, Matthew was able to understand it as a prophecy about the birth of Jesus. What he has done is, in effect, to recycle the original text and use it in a new situation.

This way of handling the text of the Old Testament is likely to make scholars blanch: by training, we have been taught to treat the text with respect, to take note of its context, to ask about what it originally meant, and not what it has been made to mean. We tend to look askance when texts are wrenched out of their original context and used in a new way. But what Matthew does with this particular text is the kind of thing that spiritual men and women, Jews and Christians, and visionaries such as poets and painters, have always done with the text: they see new meanings in it, and realize its relevance to different situations. And this is not just something that happens to the biblical text, for other texts are frequently being given a new setting. Take, for example, the song 'It's a Long Way to Tipperary'; originally a romantic love-song, sung by a lonely Irishman in London, dreaming of his home in Ireland, it was taken over by the troops in the First World War, and for most of us remains associated with men in the trenches, longing for their homes, which were anywhere but in Ireland.[10] The scriptures have been continually recycled, and what we see in the New Testament is a major recycling programme, as Christians found new meanings in old texts. There is a sense, indeed, in which we must always do this with the text if it is to speak to us in the situation in which we find ourselves. There is a very important theological principle here: on the one hand, you can treat Isaiah's words as referring to one event only – whether it is to the fate of Jerusalem in 733 BC or to the birth of Jesus; on the other, you can say that behind Isaiah's words is the conviction that God is a God who saves his people again and again, and will be with them throughout history.[11] And this, Matthew claims, is what is happening in the birth of Jesus.

On, then, to chapter 2. Jesus has been born, and *magi* come to Jerusalem from the East, looking for a child who is to be King of the Jews. The *magi* are wise men of some kind – astrologers, perhaps, since they have observed a star. Somewhat naively, they make no secret of why they have come: King Herod is alarmed, thinking that his throne is in danger. He consults Jewish scholars, who tell him that the Messiah would be born in Bethlehem. In confirmation, they refer him to a passage in the book of Micah:

'And you, Bethlehem, in the land of Judah,
are by no means least among the rulers of Judah;
for from you shall come a ruler
who is to shepherd my people Israel.'[12]

So Herod sends the *magi* to Bethlehem, with instructions to send him word when they have found the child, and they set off to Bethlehem, following the star. Arrived at their destination, the star obligingly stops at the right house, and the wise men duly worship the child and offer their gifts. This, too, though Matthew does not explicitly say so, is a fulfilment of scripture. Isaiah 60.3, describing how people will come to worship God in Jerusalem, tells how 'nations will journey towards your light, and kings to your radiance', and goes on to speak of gifts of gold and frankincense. We might think that Matthew has missed a trick in not reminding us of what the prophet says, but we shall find later on that he frequently alludes to scripture without actually quoting it. Having presented their gifts, the wise men are warned in a dream not to return to Herod, and set off home by another road.

The story, it has to be said, does not sound a very probable one. Why should these eastern *magi* have had any interest in the new king of a tiny and unimportant country like Judah? And what was the star (or was it perhaps a comet?) they were said to be following? Many attempts have been made to identify it, but stars simply do not behave in this kind of way. And even if they did, why should this one lead the *magi* to Jerusalem, rather than straight to Bethlehem? The detour to Jerusalem conveniently allows Matthew to introduce another biblical quotation, announcing that the Messiah is to be born in Bethlehem; and since Jesus is then discovered in Bethlehem, here is another assurance to us that he is in fact the promised King of the Jews. But the fact that the magi went first to Jerusalem served also to alarm Herod, with tragic consequences, since he, on discovering that he had been deceived by his visitors, sent his soldiers to kill all the young children in the Bethlehem area, so fulfilling the prophecy from Jeremiah about Rachel weeping for her children.[13] Matthew's story raises acute theological problems. One cannot help but feel that the star, however divine its origin, made a mistake in leading the wise men first to Jerusalem, for the result was the massacre of the innocents. Jesus and his parents escaped the slaughter, however, having been warned by an angel in a dream to flee to Egypt. Their flight not only saved the child's life, but enabled yet another prophecy to be fulfilled: 'Out of Egypt I have called my son.' Once again, we have a text that has clearly been recycled; originally, Hosea's words referred to the nation Israel, whom God rescued from Egypt at the Exodus;[14] but now they are used of Jesus, who is to be known as Son of God. It is not until after Herod's death, however, that Joseph has a further dream, in which an angel tells him that it is safe to return. And then, in yet another dream, he is diverted from Judaea, where Herod's son is now on the throne, and brings Jesus to Galilee, to the town of Nazareth. In this way, Matthew concludes, the words spoken through the prophets, 'He shall be called a Nazorean', have been fulfilled.

How much of this chapter is based on 'what actually happened' I do not know, and it is impossible to know. We do not know what sources Matthew was using. Asking historical questions will not get us very far. There is good reason to believe that much of his narrative here is based on legend rather than history. However, fortunately we are not concerned with asking that kind of question, but with theological questions. What we need to ask is: what is Matthew trying to tell us, here, about Jesus? What kind of information is he trying to give us?

The first, and most obvious answer, is that he is trying to impress on us the fact that everything that happens in connection with the birth of Jesus is the fulfilment of scripture: the place where Jesus is born, the flight to Egypt, the fact that he grew up in Nazareth, all are seen as foretold in scripture. The most puzzling of these three references is Nazareth, for no one has ever been able to trace the passage which Matthew claims to be quoting! Either his version of the Old Testament was slightly different from ours or he was writing from memory and has misquoted something. Nevertheless, we get the point Matthew is making: the events surrounding the birth of Jesus were all the fulfilment of scripture. And since that means that they are also the fulfilment of God's purpose, we find that angels play a frequent part in the story, making sure that Jesus is saved from any danger and that this purpose is achieved.

Even the massacre of the innocents is the fulfilment of scripture. But, we ask, how could a massacre have been part of God's plan? Why the attempt on Jesus' life? Here, too, Matthew is using these stories to make a theological point. Why should anyone try to kill Jesus? Why should his birth, itself a joyful event, bring such suffering? Matthew has already shown us that Jesus is the descendant of David, and therefore the rightful King of the Jews. But throughout these scenes there is another figure who is clearly in mind – the figure of Moses. Herod was not the first tyrant in history to have acted in this murderous way. In the book of Exodus, we read how the Egyptian Pharaoh decided to kill all the young male Israelite children. According to Jewish tradition, the reason was that he had been warned that the future liberator of the Jewish people was about to be born.[15] The Pharaoh therefore gave instructions that all baby boys should be drowned at birth. Nevertheless, of course, his attempt to prevent the fulfilment of God's plan for his people failed: God spoke to Moses' father in a dream, and when the child was born he was hidden, and then saved by the Pharaoh's own daughter.

The parallels with the story of Jesus are clear, but not exact: each child has an attempt made on his life by a wicked king; in both stories, many innocent children die as a result; in both, a divine intervention saves the child's life; Jesus, like Moses, spends his early days in Egypt; each of them has to flee from his homeland, and returns when the wicked tyrant is dead. The parallels are not accidental: in some sense, the story of Jesus' birth repeats the story of Moses. Why? The answer is that Matthew wants us to think of Jesus, not just as the son of David, and so as the Davidic Messiah, but as a new Moses, who will save his people, very much as Moses saved his people from slavery in Egypt: he is to be called Jesus, because he will save his people from their sins. That name is doubly appropriate, since the man who followed Moses and led the Israelites into the Promised Land was also named 'Joshua'.

There's a tendency among Christians to assume that messianic expectation among the Jews at the time of Jesus was cut and dried, and centred on the descendant of David. But that was only one thread in a very complex skein of expectation. Another very important hope was that God would send his people a prophet like Moses;[16] he, too, like the king, would be anointed, set apart by God for his work. We tend not to think very highly of prophets, probably because we contrast them unfavourably with Jesus. We forget just how important the prophets were – the men and women through whom God spoke and acted; and most important of all was Moses, who had brought his people out of Egypt and passed on to them the Law which God gave him on Mount Sinai. In many ways, Moses was the most significant figure in the whole history of Israel; and the events with which he was associated –

the Exodus, the Passover, the giving of the Law – were the great formative events in the life of the nation. So if Matthew is now telling us that Jesus is a 'new Moses', that is a very important piece of information to add to the other things he has told us so far.

When we were looking at Mark's introduction, I suggested that it was different in format from the rest of the Gospel: we had an Old Testament quotation, a voice from heaven, and Satan and the Holy Spirit on the stage. The material Matthew uses in his introduction is also unusual: a genealogy, angels appearing in dreams, *magi* following a mysterious star. Only the constant reference to scripture is something which is repeated, from time to time, later in the Gospel. In Mark, the information he gives us in his introduction is particularly important for understanding the rest of his story. Because we know that Jesus is the one to whom the Old Testament points forward we understand why he teaches and acts with such great authority; because we know that he has battled with Satan, we understand why he is able to exorcise unclean spirits; and because we know that he is Son of God, we realize the significance of the scene at the very end of Mark's story, when the centurion who executes Jesus exclaims in awe, 'Surely this man was the Son of God'. In the same way, the information that Matthew has given us is crucial for reading *his* story: what he has told us is meant to help us to understand his Gospel.

So why is Matthew interested in suggesting that Jesus was a figure like Moses? Read on a little in his Gospel, and you will find that the first major event in the story, following the account of the baptism and temptation, is the

Sermon on the Mount. Here Matthew gives us a long section of Jesus' teaching, far longer than anything we find in Mark. The setting, 'on the Mount', is important. In Exodus, we are told how Moses went up Mount Sinai to speak with God, came down again and told the people what God had said to him. Now Jesus speaks *from* the mountain; he sits, as a sign of his authority, and he delivers a sermon which contains remarkable echoes of the teaching of Moses. Indeed, he claims that what he is teaching is the fulfilment of the Law which Moses delivered. And yet, remarkably, it sounds at times as though he is contradicting Moses! 'You have heard it said in time past,' says Jesus, 'but I say unto you . . .'[17] But the Greek word *de*, here translated 'but', does not imply a strong contrast, and in other contexts is often translated 'and'. Moreover, if you look at the teaching in Matt. 5.21–48 carefully, you will see that there is no contradiction; rather, Jesus is pointing to the divine will behind the original Law; he fulfils the Law by filling it out. The teaching of Jesus is more penetrating than that of Moses, closer to the original, divine intent.

When I was fixing the details of this lecture course, I received a number of somewhat smudgy faxes from Victoria; sometimes my fax machine spewed out three copies of the same page, sometimes a page went missing, always the quality of the print was pretty poor. I have no doubt that what was being fed in at this end was an excellent and perfect original. The picture Matthew offers us in the Sermon on the Mount is of Jesus as the one who truly knows and teaches the will of God. What the people had had hitherto was only a poor fax copy, given through

Moses. Now they have the original, because Jesus is greater than Moses. But it is not that his teaching is a copy of that given by Moses: rather *Moses'* teaching was a copy, and *Jesus* presents us with the original.

This theme of Jesus as the great teacher is found throughout Matthew's story; no wonder, then, that the miraculous rescue of Jesus at birth should 'echo' that of Moses. The rest of Matthew's introduction also provides us with vital information for understanding his Gospel. Jesus, we have been told, is the legitimate descendant of David, and King of the Jews; the idea that Jesus is a king is taken up later in the Gospel,[18] and of course he dies as King of the Jews.[19] He was called Jesus because he will save his people from their sins – and at the end of the Gospel we learn that Jesus' blood is shed for the forgiveness of sins.[20] Jesus is acknowledged as king by foreign visitors, and worshipped by them: there are hints later in the story that although Jesus himself confines his mission to the Jewish nation, the Gentiles' opportunity to respond will come after his death.[21] The final words of the Gospel are those of the Risen Christ: 'Go to all nations and make them my disciples, teaching them to obey all the things I have commanded you.' The teaching Jesus gave is to be continued, and to be offered to Gentiles as well as Jews. The foreigners who come at the beginning of the story symbolize the members of many nations who will worship him at the end. At the very beginning, too, a wicked king, a puppet of Rome, attempted to kill Jesus; his plot points forward to the plot of the Jewish authorities against Jesus at the end of the story, and to his death at the decree of a Roman governor; both plots, however, are thwarted by

God: at the beginning, by Jesus' escape to Egypt; at the end, by his resurrection. Finally, the massacre of the innocents reminds us that even God's plan of redemption cannot be achieved without suffering; in the Gospel story this is primarily Jesus' own suffering, but in years to come it will involve the suffering of those who follow him. What we are told in these opening chapters, then, points forward to the dénouement of the story. The beginning of the story hints at the ideas which will be made plain at the end. But the end of the story will, of course, be yet another beginning, as the disciples are sent out to proclaim this gospel to the whole world.

3

A Spiritual Key: Luke 1–2

'Each venture is a new beginning'
(T.S. Eliot, *Four Quartets*, East Coker V)

The story about Jesus told by our first three evangelists, Matthew, Mark and Luke, is in many ways very similar; so much so that often we find that they use identical or almost identical wording. Only in their introductions are they strikingly different. Why? I have been suggesting that each evangelist provided us with an introduction that stressed the particular theological themes that *he* considered important, and the ideas that he wants us to look out for as we read the rest of his book.

If we ask why Luke gives us an introduction that is so very different from those of the other evangelists, then it is perhaps because he wants to stress, above all, that the Holy Spirit is at work in the ministry of Jesus and in the mission of his followers. But first, we have to decide which of Luke's introductions we are talking about.

Luke seems to have been one of those people who finds it difficult to get started: he kept on writing introductions. He reminds me of one of my research students, who has been working with me for five years, and who presents me with one paper after another, each longer than the last, and each headed 'Introduction'. *When*, I ask him, is he going to get past the introduction and into the dissertation? In fact, of course, much of the dissertation is already there, in embryo, in his introductions. And so it is with Luke.

His first introduction is very brief. It is a formal beginning: we may call it a literary introduction. In format, it is very similar to other literary introductions written at about the same time. Luke is the most polished of our New Testament writers; he writes the best Greek, and has obviously had something of a literary training, so it's not surprising to find him writing in a literary style. In the days before dust-jackets and publishers' catalogues, it was necessary to tell potential readers very quickly what kind of book it was you were writing, and explain to them why it was worth reading further. Although Luke's book is addressed to someone called 'Theophilus', he was certainly hoping for a wider audience. Luke is often described as 'the first historian of the early church', so it is not surprising if his brief preface has been compared with the introductions with which ancient historians such as Herodotus and Thucydides began their histories.[1] There are, however, other interesting parallels.[2] Here, for example, are the opening words of the so-called Letter of Aristeas, written by another Hellenistic Jew in the second or first century BC:

'Since I have collected material for a memorable history of my visit to Eleazar the high priest of the Jews, and because you, Philocrates, as you lose no opportunity of reminding me, have set great store upon receiving an

44

account of the motives and object of my mission, I have attempted to draw up a clear exposition of the matter for you, for I perceive that you possess a natural love of learning.'

Compare with this the way that Luke begins:

'Since many have undertaken to set down an orderly account of the events that have been fulfilled among us, even as they were handed on to us by those who were, from the beginning, eye-witnesses and servants of the word, I too decided, after investigating everything carefully from the very first, to set it all down in order, so that you, most excellent Theophilus, may know the truth concerning those matters about which you have been informed.'

Luke, then, is beginning his book in the conventional way. And he is making certain claims about what he is doing. He is, he says, arranging the material in order: but what kind of order? He doesn't say. It's often been assumed that he means 'chronological order', but he could just as well mean 'theological order'. We can only discover which it is by reading further. But notice already the hints in the somewhat loaded language that Luke is using. He is writing, he says, about 'the events that have been fulfilled among us'. You and I, I imagine, would have said that we were writing about events that had *happened*, or that had *taken place*: the verb 'fulfil' tells us something about the way in which Luke is viewing those events. Notice, too, how he describes the people on whose testimony he relies.

45

He doesn't suggest that they were unbiased and independent witnesses; far from it – he calls them 'eye-witnesses and servants of the word' (that is, of the gospel). Finally, Luke wants to assure Theophilus regarding the truth of the matters concerning which he has been informed: but the meaning of the word we have translated 'truth' is perhaps closer to 'reliability', or 'assurance', and the Greek verb 'to inform' is *katechein*, which gives us the noun 'catechumen', and so perhaps means 'to instruct'. Luke, then, wants Theophilus to be confident regarding the reliability of the things about which he has been instructed. What he is going to give us is clearly no ordinary history.

Luke's first, literary introduction, in 1.1–4, though it tells us his purpose in writing, is thus quite different from the introductions in Mark and Matthew which we have already considered. His equivalent to them comes next. In 1.5 he begins again, with the words 'In the days of King Herod of Judaea'. Remembering Matthew 1–2, we might expect him to launch straight away into the story of the birth of Jesus in Bethlehem; but Luke has another story to tell first, and it is the story of the birth of John the Baptist. Mark, you will remember, having informed us that he was going to describe the beginning of the gospel of Jesus Christ, was immediately side-tracked (as it might have seemed) into talking about John the Baptist; the reason, of course, was that he saw John as the forerunner and witness to Jesus. So, too, does Luke, but he traces the theme right back to the time of their conception.

So Luke's opening story concerns Zechariah, a priest, married to Elizabeth, who is barren; both are descendants of the priest Aaron, and both are getting on in years. Zechariah is in the temple, offering incense in the holy places. Enter an angel of the Lord, later identified as Gabriel, who tells Zechariah not to be afraid, announces that Elizabeth is to have a son, and instructs Zechariah to name him John. He will be filled, even before his birth, with the Holy Spirit, and his task will be to go before the Lord in the spirit and power of Elijah, to make the people ready for the Lord's coming. Zechariah, not surprisingly, is somewhat sceptical regarding this message, and asks for a sign that it is true, and as a punishment for his lack of faith, he is struck dumb – not exactly the kind of sign that he was seeking, but effective, nevertheless.

The scene changes to Galilee, where Gabriel appears again, this time to Mary, a virgin betrothed to Joseph, who is of the house of David. She is told that she, too, is to conceive and have a son, and that he is to be given the name 'Jesus'. He will be called the Son of the Most High, and he will be given the throne of his ancestor David. Like Zechariah, Mary questions the angel's message, but her response is obviously seen as positive, not negative.[3] She is told that she will conceive through the power of the Holy Spirit. She, too, is given a sign: it is the fact that her cousin Elizabeth has conceived in her old age.

It would be difficult to miss the parallelism between these two stories; they move, as it were, in tandem. Luke has obviously deliberately constructed his narrative so that we understand that from the very beginning, even before they were born, John was Jesus' forerunner, and pointed forward to him, preparing the way for the one who was to follow him.

47

Mary now comes to visit Elizabeth, and at the very moment of their meeting, the child leaps in Elizabeth's womb, acknowledging the coming of the one who follows him. Elizabeth, filled with the Holy Spirit, greets Mary with a blessing, and Mary bursts into song. We may surely assume that the Magnificat, also, is inspired by the Holy Spirit. In it, Mary extols the great things that God has done and is doing: he has shown mercy to those who fear him, and strength to those who are proud; he has brought down the mighty from their thrones and lifted up the lowly. He has filled the hungry with good things, and sent the rich away empty. He has helped his servant Israel, and remembered the promise he made to Abraham and his descendants.

In fact, of course, these accomplishments all lie in the future. What we are given is not so much an account of what God has already done, as what he is going to do through Jesus. The Magnificat is a summary of what is about to happen. The story itself also points to the future, since the central role played by the two women is a demonstration of the way in which the lowly are going to be lifted up.

Following this meeting of the two mothers we have, in turn, the accounts of the two births. Elizabeth gives birth to a son, and eight days later the child is circumcised and, to the surprise of relatives and friends, he is named 'John' by his parents. Zechariah, having obeyed the angel's command, recovers his tongue, and makes up for lost time by launching into the Benedictus. Like his wife, he too is said to be filled with the Holy Spirit. Scholars have sometimes suggested that Luke mixed up his sources at this point, because Zechariah appears to be addressing the wrong child, and is talking about Jesus rather than about John. But of course he is! John's function is to be Jesus' forerunner, and his birth is a sign of the coming birth of Jesus. The real significance of John's birth is that he is the herald of forthcoming salvation. And so we find Zechariah blessing God because he has raised up a mighty saviour for his people in the house of his servant David. Zechariah's song repeats much of what has already been said by Mary, but at the end he turns to John: 'And you, child, will be called the prophet of the Most High, for you will go before the Lord to prepare his ways . . .' That, you remember, was what Mark told us at the beginning of *his* Gospel. And the child grew, Luke tells us, and became strong in spirit.

And so John disappears from the stage and we come to the story of the birth of Jesus himself. We are told how Joseph, because he was a descendant of David, had gone to Bethlehem with Mary to register in a census. Historians can find no record of this particular census, nor of any requirement that people should have to travel to their ancestral towns to register. Luke, however, records the story as he has heard it, for it explains how Jesus, who was brought up in Nazareth, could have been born in Bethlehem, the city of David. We have already been told twice that Jesus is the promised descendant of David. Once again the angel appears, explaining the meaning of what has taken place to shepherds in the fields: 'To you is born this day in the city of David a Saviour, who is Christ, the Lord.' They, too, are given a sign that what they have been told is true: they will find the child in a manger. A chorus

49

of angels appears and confirms the message, which the shepherds themselves immediately verify.

This brief narrative echoes the information we have been given in the 'hymns' of chapter 1. But now perhaps the story itself begins to point forward to what is going to happen later. The child born on a journey, with nowhere to lie except a manger, will become the man whose whole ministry takes the form of a journey, and who has nowhere to lay his head.[4] The poverty of the circumstances surrounding Jesus' birth is matched by the humble origins of those who are summoned to see him – mere shepherds, in contrast to Matthew's wise men, who came bearing rich gifts. The poverty and humility of those who welcomed Jesus' birth is once again in keeping with a central theme of Luke's Gospel.

The story of Jesus' birth is told at greater length than that of John's, but it, too, is followed by the account of his circumcision, at which ceremony he was given the name 'Jesus', in accordance with the angel's instructions. The chapter ends with a statement similar to that about John which closes chapter 1: we are told that Jesus increased in wisdom and stature, and in favour with God and man.[5]

Luke has clearly deliberately set the stories of John and Jesus side by side. Here are two stories of remarkable births: the one, to an old, barren woman who is past the age for child-bearing; the other to a young virgin who has had no sexual relationship with a man; both births, he seems to be saying, are equally remarkable, equally impossible, unless the Spirit of God is at work. In Mark's Gospel, John bears witness to Jesus from the moment he appears in the wilderness, proclaiming a baptism of repentance, but in Luke, John bears witness to Jesus even before he is born. The parallel stories are used as a framework to give us the necessary information about who the two children are. John is the prophet who will go before the Lord to prepare his ways, but Jesus will be great, and will rule over the house of his ancestor David for ever. He is the Messiah, the Lord, and will be called Son of God; he is a Saviour, who will bring salvation to the humble and judgment to the arrogant; he will cast down the powerful and lift up the lowly. All this information is given to us in the words of angels or people inspired by the Holy Spirit, whose words are therefore reliable. Once again, we are being privileged to overhear, as it were, statements of the divine viewpoint regarding the significance of events. We will not be surprised, later in the Gospel, to find Jesus declaring that he has come to seek out and save the lost;[6] nor will we be surprised to learn that the humble and the outcast find a place in the Kingdom of God, while the arrogant and mighty are excluded.[7]

The parallels between John and Jesus inevitably run out, however, because Luke has a great deal more that he wants to tell us about the birth of Jesus. Following his circumcision, which took place on the eighth day, as the Law decreed, his parents brought Jesus to Jerusalem, to present him to the Lord, and they offered the appropriate sacrifice for purification, in accordance with what was laid down in the Law of the Lord. Three times in three verses, 2.22–24, Luke tells us that this was all done according to the Law of the Lord, and in v.39 he insists again that they did everything required by the Law of the Lord. Luke is certainly anxious to stress that Jesus was righteous in terms of the Law. When we turn to the later chapters of the Gospel, we find that Luke omits (whether deliberately or not we do not know) not only the 'antitheses' used by Matthew in the Sermon on the Mount,[8] but also the account of the discussion found in Mark and Matthew regarding the tradition of the elders;[9] perhaps this is because each of these passages *could* be interpreted as an attack by Jesus on the Law. One of the intriguing differences between Mark's story and Luke's comes in the account of the crucifixion. In Mark, at the moment of Jesus' death, the centurion declares 'This was the Son of God': Mark, we can be sure, intends us to understand those words as a declaration of faith. In Luke, however, the centurion says 'Certainly this man was innocent.' How banal! Instead of words which express the greatest truth about Jesus, we have a statement that he was innocent. But for Luke, Jesus' innocence is very important. In his second volume, the Acts of the Apostles, he refers to Jesus several times as 'the righteous one'; and here, at the very beginning of his life, we see how everything was done according to the Law. There is no foundation for the accusation that Jesus was a lawbreaker.

In the course of his story about the presentation of Jesus in the temple, Luke describes how two holy people there recognized Jesus. First Simeon, a righteous and devout man who was looking for the consolation of Israel, and who was, Luke tells us no less than three times, guided by the Holy Spirit, took Jesus in his arms and declared that he had now seen the salvation promised by God, a salvation which would bring light to the Gentiles and glory to Israel. Here we have new information to add to what we have already been given: hitherto we have been told that Jesus will bring salvation to Abraham's descendants, but now we learn that his coming will mean light for the Gentiles, as well as glory for Israel. But then, turning to Mary, Simeon tells her that a sword is to pierce her soul – an ominous reminder that this salvation will take place only through Jesus' death.

So far, Luke's 'privileged' information has pointed forward to the events that take place later in the Gospel. But what of the Gentiles? Jesus does not preach to them, and heals only one (the centurion's servant). True – but Luke has a second volume up his sleeve; and when we turn to Acts, then indeed we see that the coming of Jesus means the revelation of light to the Gentiles.

The fact that Luke wrote not just one book but two raises interesting questions about the way in which he planned his Gospel. Did he intend, from the very beginning, to write a two-part blockbuster? Or was his first book such a success that he decided to write another part, about what happened next? The Acts of the Apostles is in many ways 'the story continued'. If we look at the introduction to that book, we find Luke referring to 'the things that Jesus began to do and to teach', and we find that his followers teach and do miracles and suffer, as Jesus had done before them. But there is one new theme that dominates much of the second volume, and that is the mission to the Gentiles. Yet even that theme is there, in embryo, in the words of Simeon. I suspect, then, that Luke had it in mind to write a second volume from the very beginning.

Yet the reference to the Gentiles in Luke 2 is only a hint. To those who know Luke's second volume, with its emphasis on the church's mission to the Gentiles, it may seem paradoxical that in his prologue Luke should stress Jesus' obedience to the Law. Why is the so-called 'evangelist to the Gentiles' so Jewish? There is a certain tension between the prologue to the Gospel, with its emphasis on Jesus as a true son of Israel, on his presence in temple worship and the way in which he fulfilled Old Testament promises, and the picture in Acts of the Christian community being persuaded that the gospel should be preached to Gentiles as well as to Jews. Yet it is tension, and not contradiction: it is because Jesus is faithful and righteous that he will bring light to the Gentiles, and it is the same Holy Spirit now at work in him that will later bring Gentiles into the Christian community. The surprise (and the tragedy) is that though in Acts light is indeed taken to the Gentiles in the shape of the gospel, the Jews are shown as repeatedly rejecting it.

Luke likes parallels: we have had Zechariah and Mary, Elizabeth and Mary, John and Jesus; now we have not only Simeon but Anna. Anna, we are told, was a prophet, which means that she, too, was inspired by the Holy Spirit. Coming up to Jesus she began to praise God and to speak about Jesus to all who were looking for the redemption of Jerusalem. Even though we are not told what Anna said, we are nevertheless told what she believed. It is, of course, typical of Luke that it is a woman who plays this significant role.

The last story in chapter 2 concerns another visit to the temple, made when Jesus was twelve years old. Having celebrated the Passover, his parents set off home, not realizing that Jesus was still in the temple, engaged in discussions with those who taught there. Everyone who heard him was astonished at his understanding and his answers. Rebuked by his parents, Jesus asked them in surprise, 'Did you not know that I must be in my Father's house?' These first words of Jesus point forward to a later chapter in Luke's story, where Jesus insists that he must go to Jerusalem.[10] He spends his last week there, teaching in the temple and disputing with the religious authorities;[11] and once again, everyone who heard him was astonished by his words.

The stories about Jesus' presentation in the temple at Jerusalem and his childhood visit there for Passover are unique to Luke: here we have another theme that becomes important in Part Two. Acts is the story of how the apostles took the gospel out into the world, but the base from which they start, and to which they frequently return, is Jerusalem. The temple plays a significant role in the story, especially in the early chapters, for the followers of Jesus worship there and teach there. It is true that Stephen, the first Christian martyr, was accused by the authorities of speaking against the temple[12] and the Law, but if we look carefully at the speech he made in his defence we discover that it is not really the temple itself that he opposes, but the failure of the people to worship God, together with their failure to obey the Law. Stephen is innocent of the charge brought against him – as Jesus himself was innocent of the charges brought against *him*. For as long as they are allowed to do so, Christians continue to worship God in the temple. It is not surprising if Luke describes how Jesus himself went faithfully to the temple from the very beginning of his life. Nor are we surprised to discover that Luke's Gospel begins and ends with worship in the temple: in the opening scene (1.8–23), Zechariah offers incense in the holy place, and in the last verse (24.53) the disciples 'spent all their time in the temple praising God'.

Like Mark and Matthew, Luke has presented us, in a short space, with a great deal of information about Jesus. Like Mark, he has chosen to begin with the theme of John as the forerunner of Jesus, but like Matthew, he has begun the story with what we term 'infancy narratives'. Also like Matthew – and unlike Mark – the information is brought out into the open, and known by quite a number of people. Like both the other two evangelists, the information that he has given us points us forward to what are going to be key ideas in the rest of his story – and in his case, that means in Acts as well as the Gospel. But also like Mark and Matthew, he points us back to the past, and to God's plan for his people. Mark did this by beginning with a quotation from the Old Testament; Matthew did it by beginning with a genealogy which went back to Abraham, and with a whole series of Old Testament quotations. We may be surprised to find that Luke does not use any Old Testament quotations in his first two chapters, though there are plenty later in the Gospel and in Acts. But though there are no actual quotations, these two chapters are in fact a pastiche of Old Testament allusions, and are written in a style very reminiscent of the Old Testament. One gets the impression that he set out deliberately to write in such a way as to make people think: 'Why! This is the continuation of the story we have heard so many times of God's dealings with his people; here is the next, and crucial, chapter in the story of salvation.' If Luke in writing these chapters has one eye on the story that he is going to tell in the rest of the Gospel, of the salvation that comes through Jesus, then he certainly has the other on the story of how God saved his people in the past.

There is, however, another way in which Luke links what God has done in the past with what he does in and through Jesus and with what he does in and through his followers. Throughout these first two chapters there is repeated reference to the Holy Spirit of God. That is another vital clue to the significance of what is taking place: it is God who is at work – the God who was at work in the great events of the Old Testament story. To talk about God's 'Spirit' is really another way of talking about God at work in the world, active and dynamic. The same Spirit of God, who had acted to save his people and had inspired the prophets, is now at work in Zechariah and Elisabeth, in Mary and John, and above all in Jesus himself. One of the intriguing things about Luke is that after frequent references to the Holy Spirit in the first four chapters of his Gospel he scarcely mentions the Spirit again until Acts; like Mark and Matthew, he tells the story of Jesus in such a way as to leave us to draw our own conclusions. The explanation is probably very simple: the tradition that Luke uses of Jesus' words and deeds may well not have contained many references to the Holy Spirit. It is in his introduction that each evangelist lays his cards on the table, and provides us with the key to unlock the meaning of his story: then we are invited to hear that story in the light of what we already know. In his second volume, however, Luke has opportunity to remind us constantly that what is taking place in the life of the church is the work of the Spirit.

The theme of the Spirit continues in chapters 3 and 4. Luke, I said, had many introductions, and in 3.1 he begins another. Indeed, many scholars have argued that this is the *real* beginning of the Gospel, and that chapters 1 and 2 are a later addition. I hope by now that I will have persuaded you that they must be wrong. These first two chapters are the vital theological introduction. But 3.1 certainly marks a new beginning, for it takes up the story at the point where Mark began it, and it sets events into their historical context:

> 'In the fifteenth year of the reign of Emperor Tiberius, when Pontius Pilate was governor of Judaea, and Herod was ruler of Galilee, his brother Philip ruler of the region of Ituraea and Trachonitis, and Lysanias ruler of Abilene, during the high-priesthood of Annas and Caiaphas, the word of God came to John son of Zechariah in the wilderness . . .'

So what does Luke give us in this third introduction to his Gospel? This is the place where Mark began his story, but Luke has already given us much of the information that Mark springs on us in his opening lines. We already know that John is Jesus' forerunner, and the voice from heaven simply confirms what we have been told before. The effect, inevitably, is that this section makes far less impact than in Mark. Luke tells this part of the story with greater detail than does Mark. He quotes the passage from Isaiah at considerable length (and omits the phrases from Exodus and

Malachi), but the spotlight is on John himself rather than on the coming one. We are told more about the teaching of John the Baptist, and the kind of demands he made on his hearers: no longer is John merely a signpost pointing forward to the one who follows him. The story of Jesus' baptism is told almost incidentally, and the voice from heaven confirms what we already know – that Jesus is the Son of God. Then follows a genealogy (different from Matthew's) tracing Jesus' legal descent via Joseph through David and Abraham right back to Adam, 'son of God'. In chapter 4, the story of the Temptation is told in detail. If we look back at Matthew, we find that he does something very similar: he, too, gives a more detailed account of John's teaching, and a fuller account of the Temptation. Matthew and Luke have both provided us already with their own, distinctive, introductions, and though they have included these stories because they clearly believed them to be important parts of the tradition, neither of them needed *this* part of the narrative to set out what they believe to be the important themes of the gospel. Luke's third introduction has really become simply part of the narrative.

Nevertheless, Luke has not yet finished with introductions. Or, to be more accurate, he has not yet finished with stories which contain the germ of what is still to come. Luke 4.14 marks the beginning of Jesus' ministry:

'Then Jesus, filled with the power of the Spirit, returned to Galilee . . . And he came to Nazareth, where he had been brought up, and went, as was his custom, into the synagogue on the sabbath day. He stood up to read, and he was given the scroll of the prophet Isaiah. And he unrolled the scroll and found the place where it was written:

> "The Spirit of the Lord is upon me,
> because he has anointed me
> to bring good news to the poor.
> He has sent me to proclaim release to the captives
> and recovery of sight to the blind,
> to let the oppressed go free,
> to proclaim the year of the Lord's favour." . . .

> Then he began to say to them, "Today this scripture has been fulfilled in your hearing." '

The very first incident in Jesus' ministry, then, even before he has called any disciples, is the reading of the Old Testament, and the declaration that in reading it, and applying it to himself, it has been fulfilled. He is the one on whom God's Spirit rests, and who has been anointed by God to perform certain tasks. This passage from Isaiah 61 has become, in effect, Jesus' manifesto: this is the programme that he is now committed to undertake. His hearers are at first amazed, then scandalized. Jesus declares that no prophet is accepted in his own town, and we realize that he will not be accepted in Nazareth. He goes on to speak of Elijah, who was sent by God to lodge with a Gentile widow in Sidon, rather than with one of the many Israelite widows, and of Elisha, who cleansed the Gentile Naaman, rather than one of the many Israelite lepers. The implication is clear: it will be the Gentiles, rather than the Jews, who respond to his message. Whereupon his hearers are overcome with rage, and attempt to lynch him, but he escapes.

Once again, we see here, in embryo, ideas that are going to become important later in the Gospel; Jesus will not be accepted by his fellow townspeople – nor, indeed, by his own countrymen. It will be the Gentiles, not the Jews, who respond to the gospel, and one day his own people will engineer his death, even though, even then, he will continue on his way.

But what of his manifesto? Jesus claims that the Spirit of the Lord is upon him – something that we, though not the people in the synagogue at Nazareth, already know to be true. He claims that he has been anointed to bring good news to the poor. No sooner does he leave Nazareth than he goes throughout Galilee preaching good news; and it is the poor, the humble, the outcasts, the outsiders, who respond. He claims that he has been sent to proclaim release to the captives, and to let the oppressed go free, and in the chapters that follow we find him healing people and exorcising evil spirits. These are the captives and the oppressed, for later in the Gospel we are told that a crippled woman had been bound by Satan,[13] and that those possessed by demons are also his captives.[14]

As we read through the next three or four chapters, we find Jesus doing the various things referred to in this passage; we see him living out his manifesto. And then in chapter 7 John, now in prison, sends messengers to Jesus to ask: 'Are you the one who is to come or not?' John announced the coming one, but he does not yet know what we have known since the very beginning of the story, that the coming one is Jesus. So what does Jesus do? Send a message saying 'Yes, of course!'? No. According to Luke, the first thing he does is to heal a large number of people of various complaints and diseases and evil spirits, and to give sight to a large number of people who are blind. I am intrigued by that reference to the blind in particular, for the promise in the manifesto that Jesus is to give sight to the blind is the one item that has so far not been fulfilled. It is as though Luke, in telling the story, decided that he needed to make it clear that the whole programme had indeed been carried out. Jesus then tells the messengers, 'Go and tell John what you have seen and heard: the blind receive their sight, the lame walk, the lepers are cleansed, the deaf hear, the dead are raised, the poor have good news brought to them.' And John is left to draw his own conclusions.

So once again, in the story about Jesus at Nazareth, we have an introduction, this time to Jesus' ministry, that shows us the significance of the stories that follow – the key that unlocks the meaning of Jesus' ministry. By the time John's messengers are sent back to him, we have been given the proof that Jesus is the anointed one described in Isaiah 61, and John has been given the proof that Jesus is the one whose coming he announced.

4.14–30 really is the last of Luke's many introductions – until, that is, he comes to Volume Two! But here he gives us only a very brief introduction of five verses, before he gets launched on his story. For Volume Two, after all, he hardly needs more, since there is a sense in which the whole of the Gospel serves as an introduction to explain what happens in Acts.

A Spiritual Key: Luke 1–2

Luke, the literary man, surely knew the importance of beginnings, and he made the most of them.

4

A Glorious Key: John 1.1–18

'In my beginning is my end'

(T.S. Eliot, *Four Quartets*, East Coker I)

'In the beginning was the word.' These famous words at the beginning of the Fourth Gospel have long been recognized as the introduction to something rather special. The first eighteen verses of John are frequently spoken of as a 'prologue', and are seen as in some sense standing apart from the rest of the Gospel. But are they also the *key* to the Gospel? Do these verses serve, like the introductions to the other Gospels, to provide the reader with the vital information needed to understand the rest of the book?

These opening paragraphs of John are very different in their style from the passages that we have explored so far. Mark gave us a few crisp, dramatic scenes; Luke and Matthew, though more expansive, also provided us with introductions in narrative form. John, in contrast, offers us solid theology! Controversy has raged as to whether these first eighteen verses were an original part of the Gospel. Some scholars have argued that they are poetic in structure, and began life as a separate 'hymn' or poem. They suggest that the book originally began with the witness of John the Baptist to Jesus, and that you can begin to read the story at 1.19. Well of course you can, just as you can begin reading Mark at 1.14. But if you are so foolish as to do so, then in each case you will have thrown away the key to what follows. If we are to understand John's Gospel, we must read these eighteen verses first. What these scholars have noticed is that there is a certain 'disjunction' between John's prologue and what follows. This disjunction is not, I suggest, an indication of editing, but an inevitable feature if a 'prologue' is to fulfil its purpose; the same phenomenon occurs in the other Gospels (in particular at the end of Luke 2) and in some dramas. And why should we be surprised if John offers us a theological introduction? Mark's Gospel consists of short crisp scenes, and so does his introduction, even if these particular scenes are somewhat unusual. Matthew and Luke both give us more measured narratives throughout their Gospels, and they do the same in their introductions, even though, again, the actual stories they relate here are unusual. As for John, though his Gospel has a narrative framework, much of the book is given up to what we call 'discourses', long detailed theological statements explaining the relationship of Jesus to God and to the world. What, then, should we expect to find in his introduction *except* a theological statement?

When we come to unpack John's prologue we shall, I think, discover that, in spite of his language and style, which are so different from those of the other evangelists, he is giving us information that in many ways is very similar to that with which Mark, Matthew and Luke provided us. And one of the intriguing links comes in the opening phrase: 'In the beginning'. Mark, you remember, began his Gospel with the words 'The beginning', while

Beginnings: Keys that Open the Gospels

Matthew began with the Greek word *genesis*, meaning 'origin'. Luke, the literary man, was the exception, but even he said that what he was writing had come to him from those who had been eyewitnesses of the gospel *from the beginning*. In their different ways, all the evangelists seem to have thought that the beginning was important. John is certainly no exception.

'In the beginning': the phrase in Greek consists of only two words, in Hebrew of only one, and it is the word with which the book of Genesis begins. Genesis 1 tells us what happened in the beginning, when God said 'let there be light', and there was light, and he separated the light from the darkness; he went on, we are told, to create the heavens and the earth and to bring forth life from the earth. There are many echoes of this story in the opening verses of John 1 (in the beginning, God, the word, life, light, darkness), and it seems that the passage is in fact what is known as a *midrash* – that is an exposition – of those opening words of Genesis; similar expositions of a biblical text are known in Jewish writings dating from about the same time.[1]

Already we have found another link between our four introductions. All four begin with what happened in the Old Testament. Mark found the beginning of the gospel about Jesus in the promises of God in the Old Testament. Matthew began by tracing the genealogy of Jesus back to Abraham: the purpose of God for his people went right back to the founder of the race. Quotations from the Old Testament hammered home the message that what was happening was the will of God. Luke, the literary man, who could write in the most polished style, chose to write

66

his opening chapters in the style of the Old Testament, as though to show that his story is the continuation of a story that had begun right back with Adam, to whom he traces the line of Jesus' descent. And now John begins with a phrase from Genesis 1.1, and so takes us right back to the beginning of time, before the creation of the world. In pointing us to the Old Testament, all four evangelists are pointing us to the purpose of God, who is at work in creation, active in history, and revealed in scripture.

God is at work in creation. The other evangelists stress this by talking about the Spirit of God. In Mark, you remember, the Spirit of God was referred to three times in the first thirteen verses: in the rest of his story we see that Spirit at work in Jesus, destroying evil and creating new life. In Matthew and Luke, Jesus is conceived through the Holy Spirit. Luke's story was full of references to the Spirit, confirming that what was taking place in the birth of Jesus was due to the creative Spirit of God; and in his first sermon in Nazareth, Jesus claimed that the Spirit was at work in him. John alone makes no reference to the Holy Spirit – though we shall find a very important reference when he begins his narrative. In his own way, however, he is telling us the same thing, for talking about 'the Holy Spirit' is only another way of talking about God at work in the world; and that is certainly what he is describing here, although instead of talking about the Holy Spirit, John talks about 'the Word', through whom everything was made.

To understand these opening verses of John 1, therefore, we need to compare them with the first five verses of Genesis 1:

'In the beginning, God created the heavens and the earth. The earth was a formless void, and darkness covered the deep; and the Spirit of God hovered over the surface of the water. Then God said, "Let there be light," and there was light; and God saw that the light was good, and he separated light from darkness.'

'In the beginning was the Word, and the Word was with God, and the Word was God. He was with God in the beginning. All things came into being through him, and without him nothing came into being. What came into being in him was life, and that life was the light of all people. The light shines in the darkness, and the darkness has never overcome it.'

With that reference to the light shining in the darkness, we link the theme of creation with the idea that God continues to reveal himself to his people in history and through the prophets, who speak in his name. In letting light shine he reveals himself, shows them his glory. As we read on through John's Gospel, we shall find these words triumphantly fulfilled in Jesus' death, where the light shines in the darkness, but the darkness is unable to overcome it. The struggle of darkness to overcome light reminds us again of incidents in the other Gospels' introductions: in Mark, Jesus' temptation by Satan; in Matthew, Herod's attempt to kill Jesus; and in Luke, Simeon's reference to Jesus' death.[2] But so far John has not mentioned Jesus: how do we know that what he is saying about the Word has anything to do with him? At this point there enters a familiar figure. It is, of course, none other than John the Baptist, who was also the first significant person to be mentioned in both Mark and Luke, and what we are told about him sounds very familiar:

'There was a man sent from God, whose name was John. He came as a witness to testify to the light, so that through him everyone might believe. He was not himself the light; he came to bear witness to the light.'

Once again, as in the other Gospels, John's function is to point forward to someone else, whom so far we know only as word, life and light.

As abruptly as John entered, so he disappears. The evangelist goes back to telling us about the true light which was coming into the world, but which the world did not recognize; who came to his own people, but was not accepted by them. If we have read the other Gospels, as well as their introductions, we know that Jesus is not recognized or accepted by his people. And because we know their stories, we are already thinking 'He's talking about Jesus.' But the Fourth Evangelist has still not named Jesus. What he says about people failing to recognize or accept the light is in fact just as true of the revelation of God to his people in the past; what is said about the Word applies to the beginning of time, to God's revelation in the Law and through the prophets, and to the story of Jesus which the evangelist is about to tell us. The story of Jesus is part of a story that began with creation and has been going on ever since. From the beginning of time the light has shone in the darkness and the darkness has tried to extinguish it. Even when the true light comes into the world, his own refuse to receive him. Nevertheless, there are those who do accept him and who, by believing on his name, become children of God. The light shines on in the darkness, and the darkness does not overcome it.

> 'And so the Word became flesh, and made his home among us, and we saw his glory, such glory as befits the Father's only Son, full of grace and truth.'

This time we really must be talking about Jesus, and about Jesus alone – though he still hasn't been named. And as though to confirm it, John the Baptist appears once again:

> 'John bore witness to him and proclaimed: "this is the man of whom I said, 'He comes after me, but ranks ahead of me,' for he existed before me."'

Now these two appearances of John the Baptist are decidedly odd, for in the middle of a passage of profound theology, they bring us down to earth with a bump. They are also quite different in style from the rest of the passage. The prologue as a whole is often described as a poem, and though it is not always easy to say what is and what is not poetry, these lines certainly are written in an exalted style, whereas the statements about John are definitely prose. So what are they doing here? One scholar described them as 'rude interruptions',[3] and thought they had been inserted when the prologue was added to the Gospel. But if the prologue was composed at the same time as the Gospel, that cannot be the explanation. So why should the author have broken into his theological introduction with these down-to-earth references to John? The answer, I suggest, is that they serve to tell us *who it is* that the evangelist is talking about. He has, you remember, been talking about the Word, and even though he has now told us that the Word became flesh, he still hasn't mentioned Jesus by name. But already we know that John bore witness to someone, and declared that the one who followed him was greater than he was. So when, in the story, we find John doing these things, we, the readers of the prologue, will know that the person he is singling out is none other than the Word made flesh. And that is precisely what happens: in 1.19–28, John is asked who he is, and he replies, 'I am a voice crying in the wilderness, nothing more; but someone else is coming after me who is much greater than I am.' And then, in the next verse, Jesus appears, and John declares 'That's him! He is the Lamb of God! I have seen the Spirit come down on him, and know that he is the one who is to baptize with the Holy Spirit.'[4]

John, then, has exactly the same function in the prologue of the Fourth Gospel as in Mark's and Luke's introductions: he is a human signpost, who points to Jesus and assures us that this is the person about whom we have heard these great theological truths.

The prologue began, I suggested, with an exposition of Genesis 1.1–5. It ends with an exposition of Exodus 33.[5] This is the story of how Moses, on Mount Sinai, asks God to grant him a favour and show him his glory. We need to understand that the Hebrew word for 'favour' is often translated by the Greek word *charis*, meaning 'grace', and that the word 'glory' is a way of referring to what someone essentially is – to his or her character, which is revealed in the face. The favour Moses requests is thus to know what the Lord is like. Moses is told that he cannot see God's face and live, but that the Lord will hide him in a cave and pass by the mountain, and Moses will be allowed to see his back, and so, as it were, have a glimpse of the reflection of his glory. This is what duly happens, and as the Lord passes by, he tells Moses what kind of God he is – compassionate and gracious, faithful and true – and he then delivers to Moses the two tablets with the ten commandments inscribed on them. So Moses is given some insight into the character of God. Moses then comes down the mountain with the Law, and his face is aglow with reflected glory, because he has been in the presence of God.

Israel, then, saw in Moses' face the reflection of God's glory; Israel heard, at second-hand, the commandments of God. We turn back to John 1, and discover that something much greater has now occurred:

> 'And the Word became flesh, and made his home among us, and we have seen his glory, the glory that belongs to the Father's only Son, full of grace and truth.'

In verse 1 we were told that the Word was God; now we are told that this Word has become flesh and made his home among us, or was present among us – the Greek verb *skenoō* used here echoes the Hebrew word *shekinah*, which is the term used of God's presence. And we have seen his glory, full of grace and truth, which are the essential qualities of God. And because we have seen the glory of the Word made flesh, we have seen the glory of God himself, for the only Son shares the character of his

72

Father. Moses was told what God was like, but the only Son has seen God face to face, and this is why he is able to reveal his nature to men and women.

> 'From his fullness we have all received, grace upon grace (or favour upon favour). No one has ever seen God (not even Moses); but the unique one, who is God, and who is in the bosom of the Father, has made him known.'

The grace (or favour) that comes to us through the Son is far greater than the favour shown to Moses, for in the Son we have been shown the full glory or nature of God. And just in case we still haven't got the point of what the evangelist is telling us, he spells it out in v.17:

> 'The Law was given through Moses; grace and truth came through Jesus Christ.'

What we have in Jesus, then, is not just a report of what God said to Moses on Mount Sinai, not just the reflection of his glory, but the embodiment of that Word and that glory: we have what the evangelist calls 'the Word made flesh', making his home among us.

We have come to the end of the Johannine prologue. What have we learned? We know that what has taken place in the person of Jesus is a *continuation* of the divine activity and divine revelation which began 'in the beginning', before creation: it is the same Word, who spoke at the beginning, on Mount Sinai and through the prophets, who has now come to live among us. We know nothing about Jesus' Davidic descent, but we do know about his divine origin. We know that his relationship to God is like that of a son to his father; and we know that the revelation that comes in Jesus is superior to the Law given to Moses, because it is a direct and perfect replica of the divine glory, not a poor copy – an idea that we found also in Matthew, in his account of the Sermon on the Mount. We know, too, that his own people, to whom he came, rejected him: nevertheless, the light shone on in the darkness, and the darkness could not overcome it.

All this is, in fact, precisely the information we need if we are going to make sense of the rest of John's Gospel. Imagine for a moment that the first page of the Gospel had been lost. Imagine that you know nothing at all about the figure of Jesus. And now imagine that you are reading John's Gospel, minus these first eighteen verses, for the first time. What are you to make of his story? I suspect that you would be just as bewildered as you would be if you were to try reading Mark's story without the first thirteen verses. In both cases, you would find yourself asking 'Who is this man? How is he able to do the things that he is said to be doing? What is going on?' But there is one major difference between the story as Mark tells it and the story told by the Fourth Evangelist. In Mark, Jesus makes no claims for himself; he tells no one who he is, and he frequently silences those people who begin to guess at the truth about him. In the Fourth Gospel, Jesus makes the most stupendous claims. He speaks openly of himself as 'the Son'; he boldly declares himself to be various things, in sentences beginning with the words 'I am . . .': 'I am the light of the world';[6] 'I am the resurrection and the life';[7]

even 'Before Abraham was, I am'.[8] At a human level, these are all outrageous claims. It is only because you and I have read the prologue that we are not shocked by them. But the characters in the story have not read the prologue and, not surprisingly, most of them are appalled by his words: 'Who is this?' they ask, and 'Who does he think he is?'

At the historical level, you may find these very different portraits of Jesus puzzling. It is impossible to reconcile a picture of him being reluctant to talk about his own identity – and even going out of his way to conceal it – with the extraordinary claims he makes for himself in the Fourth Gospel. At the *historical* level, the Jesus of the Synoptic Gospels is more believable than the Jesus described by John. But that does not mean that John's Jesus is any less authentic. It is easy to see what has happened. *All* the evangelists are presenting us with 'gospel', or 'good news'. They want to persuade us that the Christian interpretation of what Jesus did and said – that is, that God was at work in him – is the correct one. All of them, as we have seen, do that by giving us key information in their introductions, and then telling the story of Jesus. As we read that story, we realize that there are different ways of interpreting it: we can accept the evangelist's version, or we can say, with Jesus' enemies, that he is a blasphemer and that his powers come from Satan. From time to time the evangelists give us hints as to the way *they* think we should be interpreting the story. But when we come to the Fourth Gospel, the hints have become overwhelming. Whereas in the other Gospels Jesus made only implicit claims about his identity, in *this* Gospel explicit claims are put into his mouth. From time to time in John's narrative we find theological statements attributed to Jesus, which then merge into statements which are clearly those of the evangelist. We today are so eager to know the 'actual words' of Jesus that we find this method disconcerting, but we have to realize that it is in no way meant to deceive: what the Fourth Evangelist has done is to point out what he believed to be the true significance of Jesus, and to relate that significance to the situation in which he himself was writing. So we find Jesus saying boldly 'I am the light of the world', 'I am the resurrection and the life'. But the bolder the claim, the more need there is for us to have read the prologue; for without understanding that, any reader is likely to dismiss these claims as megalomania.

Jesus, then, is the Word, in whom is life, and that life is the light of all people. 'The light shines in the darkness, and the darkness has never overcome it', even though his own people, to whom he came, refused to receive him. The story of Jesus is told in the Fourth Gospel against a background of conflict. In the Synoptic Gospels, Jesus met with occasional opposition from the scribes and Pharisees; then, when he came to Jerusalem, he met hostility from the chief priests as well. But in John, Jesus meets hostility throughout his whole ministry. His opponents are normally referred to as 'the Jews' – a strange term to use, we might think, since Jesus and his disciples were all Jews. But the way the evangelist tells the story reflects the tensions of his own day, at the end of the first century AD. By the time that he is writing, the dispute between those Jews who believe in Jesus as the Messiah and those who reject the claims that his followers make on his behalf has come to a head. The conversations in his Gospel between Jesus and 'the Jews' reflect the furious debates between Christians and their fellow-Jews about who Jesus is. On the one hand, the followers of Jesus were claiming that what he did and said was nothing less than the works and words of God himself; on the other, their opponents dismissed such claims as blasphemous. Throughout the Gospel, the Jews are depicted as rejecting Jesus and failing to understand him. The reason for their failure is that they do not comprehend the truths spelled out for us in the prologue: they do not recognize Jesus' divine origins.

We are accustomed to thinking of Christianity as a new and separate religion, but our New Testament documents were written at a time when Christians were still very conscious of their faith as the fulfilment of Judaism. What we have in the Fourth Gospel is very much in the nature of a family squabble; and as in so many family squabbles, what the parties are quarrelling about is their inheritance. To which of them does it belong? 'To us, of course,' said the Jews. 'We are Abraham's children; we listen to Moses, and obey his commandments.' 'Nonsense!' said the Christians. 'If you were Abraham's children, you would be doing the things that Abraham did.'[9] 'If you believed Moses, you would believe Jesus, for Moses wrote about him.'[10] Audaciously, the Christians were claiming that it was they, and not the orthodox Jews, who were the true children of Abraham; they who had really understood the writings of Moses. And underlying many of these disputes are some of the themes that have already been highlighted in the prologue: light,[11] life,[12] and truth.[13]

Beginnings: Keys that Open the Gospels

We shall perhaps understand what is going on behind the pages of the Fourth Gospel if we think of it as a gigantic take-over battle. The old, established firm is Judaism. The newcomers are the Christians, and they lay claim to everything within Judaism. But the basis of their claim is, as it were, that the original founder of the firm had intended them to take it over, and that the previous team, who had been running the firm, had merely been put in as caretakers, until the time was ripe for their successors to take over.

They lay claim to everything within Judaism: and that means, above all, to the Torah, the 'Teaching' or Law, given to Moses. In one of the first controversies in the Gospel, Jesus is said to have claimed that Moses wrote about him.[14] This, of course, is what our other evangelists have claimed by quoting from the Old Testament. It is what Jesus himself is said to have claimed, in Matthew 5.17, when he declared that he had come to fulfil the Law and the prophets. But John spells out the meaning of that fulfilment in a slightly different way. It is not just that particular passages from the Old Testament are applied to Jesus – in the way, for example, that we found Matthew doing in his first two chapters. Rather the whole purpose of the Law finds its fulfilment in Jesus. It is intriguing to discover that many of the nouns used in those famous 'I am' sayings were used already in Judaism to describe the Law. 'I am the Bread, the Light, the Life, the Way, the Truth': all these terms have been used of the Jewish scriptures. And now John tells us that Jesus is claiming to *be* these things. But of course! For if Jesus is the true revelation of who God is, and not just the written copy

78

given to Moses, then he must be all that was ever claimed for the Law and far more. John believes that if the Jews would only read their scriptures diligently, they would discover that they witness to Jesus.[15] We who have read the prologue know already that Jesus is light and life and truth, and we understand.

These claims about who Jesus is are, moreover, backed up by actions. The 'I am' sayings are normally found in conjunction with miracles which correspond with the claims. Jesus' claim to be living bread[16] is found in a sermon following the miracle of the feeding of a large crowd of people. His claim to be the light of the world[17] is followed by the gift of sight to a man who was born blind.[18] His claim to be the door of the sheepfold and the good shepherd who lays down his life for his sheep[19] points forward to his crucifixion. His claim to be the resurrection and the life[20] follows the raising of Lazarus from the dead. But because Jesus' oponents have failed to listen to God's Word in the past, they fail to recognize that Word in the person of Jesus, even though he speaks God's words and does his works.[21]

The theme of John's prologue is the Word, which brings life and light to the world; but for God, to speak is to do, and so we are not surprised to find that his Word is revealed in *action* as well as in *speech*. The theme of the Fourth Gospel is the words and works of Jesus, which bring light and life, and which are, in fact, none other than the words and works of God himself, and so a manifestation of his glory.

'And the Word became flesh, and made his home among

us, and we saw his glory, such glory as befits the Father's only Son, full of grace and truth.'

Glory because, of course, as we have already noted, glory is a way of referring to what someone essentially is. The Word made flesh reveals the glory of the Word which is God. There is a sense in which the whole of John's Gospel is about God's glory, revealed in Jesus. But that means also that God is glorified through what Jesus does, and when God is glorified, he is truly acknowledged for what he is.

Jesus is seen as the 'fulfilment' of the Law and the prophets. But Jewish faith was expressed, not in obedience to the Law alone, but in the worship of God, which was focused on certain festivals. Now one of the interesting things about John's Gospel is that the outline of his story is very different from that followed by the other three evangelists. True, the story of Jesus' death and resurrection comes, inevitably, at the end; but before that, the setting is often very different. Instead of being based in Galilee, Jesus spends much of his time in Jerusalem, and he makes several visits there, instead of just the one. In the Synoptic Gospels, we hear about just one celebration of the Passover, the one at which Jesus dies. John mentions three Passovers, and various other festivals in between; moreover, these various festivals seem to play an important role in the telling of the story, for we find that many of the words and miracles of Jesus are appropriate to the theme of the particular festival at which they take place. Around the time of the second Passover mentioned by John,[22] for example, Jesus feeds a large crowd of people, and speaks about the theme of bread. Further, he contrasts the bread which God gave to the people in the wilderness through Moses with the bread which he himself offers them: the bread which is himself, since, he says, 'I am the bread of life'.[23] The contrast between Moses and Jesus would, of course, have seemed outrageous to any orthodox Jew; having read the statement in the prologue that the Law came through Moses, and grace and truth through Christ, you and I understand it. And the claim that Jesus himself is living bread is an appropriate one to be thinking of at Passover, which is linked with the Exodus and the gift of manna in the wilderness. Other festivals that John specifically mentions are Tabernacles[24] and the Feast of Dedication.[25] On each morning of the Feast of Tabernacles, there was a ceremony in which water was taken from the fountain at Siloam into the Temple and poured out on the altar; sure enough, we find Jesus talking of himself as the source of living water.[26] Dedication was the festival that celebrated the reconsecration of the Temple; why then should Jesus speak at this festival of giving his life for his sheep? We already know from the so-called cleansing of the temple, which is placed by John at Jesus' first visit to Jerusalem, that the temple stands as a symbol for his body, and that a new temple is to be built through his death and resurrection. Put the two ideas together, and one gets a somewhat mixed metaphor: the sheep would need a new fold rather than a new temple! But the theme of Jesus' death is certainly appropriate to the theme of the festival.

Jesus, then, is the fulfilment of all the festivals, the one through whom God is truly worshipped and glorified. Once again, we who have read the prologue should not be surprised, for we already know that in Jesus we have seen the glory of God revealed, and that means not only that in him we see what God is like, but that he is the one who truly glorifies God.

For this evangelist, however, the revelation of divine glory is focused on one event in particular: on the cross. The fact that Christians cheerfully sing the hymn 'In the cross of Christ I glory' without batting an eyelid shows the extent to which we have forgotten just how extraordinary it is to speak of a crucifixion in terms of glory. Crucifixion was designed to bring shame and humiliation, as well as excruciating pain, to its victim, and 'glory' was perhaps the most inappropriate word that could have been chosen to describe it. Luke, more logically, speaks of Jesus enduring suffering *before* he entered into glory.[27] But in John, the two themes have been coalesced. John plays on the *double entendre* in the verb 'to lift up': Jesus is lifted up to glory at the same time that he is lifted up on the cross.[28] When John speaks about Jesus or God being glorified, he is more often than not referring to Jesus' death.[29] The reason is that the cross is the supreme revelation of the nature of God: the supreme revelation of his love, and of his purpose to save the world. And because God's nature is revealed in the cross, it is by the cross that he is glorified.[30] Although Jesus reveals God's glory throughout his ministry, he does so above all in his death. The final and ultimate revelation of glory, therefore, comes at the end of the story. Everything has led up to this and pointed forward to it, from the moment that John the Baptist first pointed to Jesus and declared 'There is the Lamb of God, who takes away the sin of the world.'[31] The hour of Jesus' death is the hour for which he has been waiting, and the reason for his coming.[32]

In his unique introduction, this evangelist has given us the key that enables us to understand his Gospel. If we accept his affirmation that the Word which spoke at the very beginning of time, and which has spoken throughout history, has now become flesh in the person of Jesus, then we will understand that Jesus' words and his works are the works of God himself. The light which shone in the darkness at the creation of the world, and which has shone throughout history in God's self-revelation to his people, has shone in the life and death of Jesus, and the darkness has been unable to quench it. And it is in his last, triumphant work on the cross that, paradoxically, the glory of God is revealed in its fullness. In John, Jesus' last words before his death are a triumphant cry of triumph: 'It is accomplished!' It is in the cross, above all, that we see the glory that belongs also to the Father's only Son, here that we acknowledge him to be the embodiment of grace and truth. The evangelist's opening paragraphs find their fulfilment in Jesus' 'glorious' death.

Epilogue

For all the similarities of their accounts, our four evangelists offer us four very different interpretations of the
gospel. Nevertheless, each author is attempting to do the
same thing – namely, to present the good news about Jesus
through an account of his ministry, death and resurrection. One feature that they have in common is that each of
them begins with an introduction or 'prologue', which in a
sense stands apart from what follows, and yet is an essential part of the book. The information offered us in these
four introductions is remarkably similar. And yet how
different they are! And in what very different ways the
information is provided! In Mark, it is given through
scenes which lead straight into Jesus' ministry; in
Matthew, through a genealogy, birth narratives and
frequent references to scripture; in Luke, through a very
different set of birth narratives and prophetic comments;
in John through theological reflection. If these 'prologues'
are keys to the Gospels, then, it is essential to have the
right key. The one Mark provides will be little use for
understanding John and *vice versa*. Matthew's birth narratives suit *his* purposes, not Luke's, and Luke's account will
not help us to understand Matthew's purposes.

Epilogue

There is a sense, perhaps, in which our evangelists have been too successful. We have used the material they supplied in their introductions to illuminate the rest of the story, and then forgotten that what they gave us there was 'privileged information', standing apart from what follows. As a result, we have been puzzled by the fact that the characters in the story could not see what appeared so obvious to us, and we have blamed them for their failure to comprehend. We have forgotten that they did not know what we know – that Jesus was Messiah, Son of God, the fulfilment of Old Testament hopes and promises, and the one in whom God's Spirit was at work. Perhaps this was inevitable: Christians who have read the story many times cannot read it except with the benefit of hindsight. We know that the strange preacher and healer wandering round Galilee is the longed-for Messiah; we share with the Fourth Evangelist the knowledge that the stupendous claims made about Jesus are true because he is the Word made flesh and the Father's only Son. With the exception of John 1.1–18, which is so obviously theological reflection, we read the prologues as though they were simply part of the narrative, and ignore their special function, which is to inform and illumine everything else.

I trust that these brief studies will help more readers to comprehend what our evangelists were doing when they offered us these keys with which to unlock the mysteries of their books, and thus to appreciate better the story that they told and the message they were attempting to convey.

85

For Further Reading

General Books

Davies, Margaret, *Matthew*, JSOT Press 1993

Green, Joel B., *The Theology of the Gospel of Luke*, Cambridge University Press 1995

Hooker, Morna D., *The Message of Mark*, Epworth Press 1983

Kingsbury, Jack Dean, *Matthew as Story*, Fortress Press ²1988

Lightfoot, R.H., *The Gospel Message of St. Mark*, Oxford University Press 1950

Lindars, Barnabas, *John*, New Testament Guides, JSOT Press 1990

Luz, Ulrich, *The Theology of the Gospel of Matthew*, Cambridge University Press 1995

Marshall, I.H., *Luke: Historian and Theologian*, Paternoster Press 1970

Moloney, Francis J., *Beginning the Good News*, St Paul Publications 1992

Richardson, Neil, *The Panorama of Luke*, Epworth Press 1982

Riches, John, *Matthew*, New Testament Guides, JSOT Press 1996

For Further Reading

Smalley, S. S., *John: Evangelist and Interpreter*, Paternoster Press 1978

Smith, D. Moody, *The Theology of the Gospel of John*, Cambridge University Press 1995

Telford, W.R., *Mark*, New Testament Guides, JSOT Press 1995

Tuckett, C.M., *Luke*, New Testament Guides, JSOT Press 1996

More technical studies

Alexander, Loveday, *The Preface to Luke's Gospel: Literary convention and social context in Luke 1.1–4 and Acts 1.1*, SNTS Monograph 78, Cambridge University Press 1993

—, 'Luke's Preface in the Context of Greek Preface-Writing', *Novum Testamentum* 28, 1986, 48–74

Barrett, C.K., 'The Prologue of St John's Gospel', in *New Testament Essays*, SPCK 1972, 27–48

Bilezikian, G.G., *The Liberated Gospel: A Comparison of the Gospel of Mark and Greek Tragedy*, Baker Book House 1977

Borgen, Peder, 'Observations on the Targumic Character of the Prologue of John', *New Testament Studies* 16, 1970, 288–95

Brown, Raymond E., *The Birth of the Messiah*, Geoffrey Chapman ²1993

Earl, D., 'Prologue-form in Ancient Historiography', *Aufsteig und Niedergang der Römischen Welt* 1.2, 1972, 842–56

Farris, Stephen, *The Hymns of Luke's Infancy Narratives*, JSNT Supplement 9, JSOT Press, 1985

Hooker, Morna D., 'John the Baptist and the Johannine Prologue', *New Testament Studies* 16, 1970, 354–8

Hooker, Morna D., 'The Johannine Prologue and the Messianic Secret', *New Testament Studies* 21, 1974, 40–58

—, 'The Beginning of the Gospel', in *The Future of Christology: Essays in honor of Leander E. Keck*, ed. Abraham J. Malherbe and Wayne A. Meeks, Fortress Press 1993, 18–28

Johnson, Marshall D., *The Purpose of the Biblical Genealogies*, SNTS Monograph 8, Cambridge University Press ²1988

Keck, L.E., 'The Introduction to Mark's Gospel', *New Testament Studies* 12, 1966, 352–70

Laurentin, René, *Structure et Théologie de Luc I–II*, Gabalda 1957

Minear, Paul S., 'Luke's Use of the Birth Stories', in *Studies in Luke–Acts*, ed. L.E. Keck and J.L. Martyn, Abingdon Press 1966 and SPCK 1968, 111–30

Oliver, H.H., 'The Lucan Birth Stories and the Purpose of Luke–Acts', *New Testament Studies* 10, 1964, 202–16

Rhoads, David and Michie, Donald, *Mark as Story*, Fortress 1982

Robinson, John A.T., 'The Relation of the Prologue to the Gospel of St John', *New Testament Studies* 9, 1963, 120–9, reprinted in *Twelve More New Testament Studies*, SCM Press 1984, 65–76

Smith, Dennis E. (ed.), 'How Gospels Begin', *Semeia* 52, Society for Biblical Literature 1991

Stendahl, K., 'Quis et Unde?', reprinted in *The Interpretation of Matthew*, ed. G.N. Stanton, T. & T. Clark ²1995, 56–66

Notes

Introduction

1. This was first pointed out by Paul Schubert, in *The Form and Function of the Pauline Thanksgivings*, BZNTW 20, 1939. I have recently applied this idea in '1 Thessalonians 1.9–10: A Nutshell – But What Kind of Nut?', in *Geschichte – Tradition – Reflexion: Festschrift für Martin Hengel zum 70. Geburtstag, III: Frühes Christentum*, ed. Hermann Lichtenberger, Mohr (Siebeck) 1996, 435–48.

1. A Dramatic Key: Mark 1.1–13

1. Aristotle, *Poetics* 10–11, 18.
2. Aristotle, *Poetics* 12.
3. Aristotle, *Rhetoric* III.14.
4. Mark 8.27–30.
5. For a discussion of the idea of Mark's Gospel as a drama see the literature cited in M.D. Hooker, 'The Beginning of the Gospel'.
6. E.g. a nurse in Euripides' *Medea*, and a peasant in his *Electra*.
7. E.g. the chorus of Persian Elders in Aeschylus' *The Persians*.

8. See Euripides' *Hippolytus*, where the opening words are spoken by Aphrodite, and *Ion*, where they are found in the mouth of Hermes.

9. See, e.g., Keck, 'The Introduction to Mark's Gospel'. The translators of the NRSV have followed this suggestion, and left a gap in the text after v.15.

10. Ex. 23.20; Mal. 3.1; Isa. 40.3.

11. Mark 9.13.

12. See M.D. Hooker, *The Signs of a Prophet*, SCM Press and Trinity Press International 1997, 9–13, 24–31.

13. Mark 9.7.

14. Rom. 6.3.

15. Mark 10.38.

2. *A Prophetic Key: Matthew 1–2*

1. See, e.g., Kingsbury, *Matthew as Story*, 43–5.

2. *The New Testament and Psalms: An Inclusive Version*, Oxford University Press, New York 1995.

3. Genesis 38.

4. Joshua 2.

5. II Sam. 11.2–5.

6. Ruth 3.

7. There is an interesting parallel between what Matthew tells us here, in his first chapter, and what Paul sums up in a couple of lines in Rom. 1.3f., where he tells his readers that the gospel of Jesus Christ is about God's Son, who was born of the seed of David according to the flesh, and declared Son of God according to the Holy Spirit by the resurrection from the dead. Notice, however, the differences between them: for Paul, Jesus' Davidic descent is apparently

physical, and his divine Sonship (or rather its declaration!) is linked with his resurrection, while for Matthew, both ideas are associated with Jesus' birth.

8. Isa. 7.14.
9. Circa 733 BC.
10. I owe this illustration to my husband. See David Stacey, *Isaiah 1–39*, Epworth Press 1993, 58.
11. Cf. Paul's contrast between 'letter' and 'spirit' in II Corinthians 3.
12. Micah 5.2. The last line comes from II Sam. 5.2.
13. Jer. 31.15.
14. Hos. 11.1.
15. Josephus, *Antiquities* II, 205.
16. Deut. 18.18.
17. Matt. 5.21f., 27f., 31f., 33f., 38f., 43f.
18. Matt. 13.41; 16.28; 20.21; 21.5; 25.34, 40.
19. Matt. 27.11, 29, 37, 42.
20. Matt. 26.28.
21. Matt. 8.11; 12.18, 21; 25.31–46. Matt. 21.43 and 22.8–10 may refer to Gentiles.

3. *A Spiritual Key: Luke 1–2*

1. Whether or not it is appropriate to describe Luke as an historian is a matter of debate. Certainly it is an inadequate description. See the discussion in Marshall, *Luke: Historian and Theologian*.
2. D. Earl, 'Prologue-form in Ancient Historiography', suggested that the model for these verses is to be found in the introductory lines of *The Iliad* and *The Odyssey*. Loveday Alexander, however, *The Preface to Luke's Gospel* and 'Luke's Preface', places Luke's prefaces in what she terms the 'scientific tradition'.

3. Moloney, *Beginning the Good News*, 110, suggests that the explanation is to be found in the form of their questions. Mary (reasonably enough!) asks how it is possible for her to conceive; Zechariah asks how he may *know* that the angel's message is true. There is, however, little difference in substance between the two reactions, and both Zechariah and Mary are given signs by the angel to demonstrate the truth of his words. On the inappropriateness of asking for a sign, see M.D. Hooker, *The Signs of a Prophet*, SCM Press Ltd and Trinity Press International 1997, 17–34.

4. Luke 9.58.

5. Luke 2.52. A similar statement is made about Jesus in v.40.

6. Luke 19.10.

7. Luke 4.16–20; 5.29–32; 6.20–26; 14.7–24.

8. Matt. 5.21–48.

9. Matt.15.1–20; Mark 7.1–23.

10. Luke 9.51; 13.33.

11. Luke 19.45–21.38.

12. One of the interesting features of Luke's Gospel is that he does not record the charge brought against Jesus by the religious authorities, in which they accused him of threatening to destroy the temple (cf. Matt. 26.59–63 and Mark 14.55–61). Has he deliberately omitted the suggestion that Jesus attacked the temple?

13. Luke 13.10–17.

14. Luke 11.14–23.

4. *A Glorious Key: John 1.1–18*

1. P. Borgen, *Bread From Heaven*, Brill 1965; 'Observations on the Targumic Character of the Prologue of John'.
2. Mark 1.12f.; Matt. 2.13–18; Luke 2.35.
3. J.A.T. Robinson, 'The Relation of the Prologue to the Gospel of St John'.
4. See M.D. Hooker, 'John the Baptist and the Johannine Prologue'.
5. See M.D. Hooker, 'The Johannine Prologue and the Messianic Secret', 52–8.
6. John 8.12.
7. John 11.25.
8. John 8.58.
9. John 8.39.
10. John 5.46.
11. John 3.19–21; 8.12ff.; 9.5, 39.
12. John 3.15, 36; 5.24–6; 6.51f.
13. John 3.33; 8.44–46; 18.37f.
14. John 5.46.
15. John 5.39.
16. John 6.35, 48, 51.
17. John 8.12; 9.5.
18. John 9.
19. John 10.7, 9, 11, 14.
20. John 11.25.
21. John 5.36–38.
22. John 6.4.
23. John 6.35.
24. John 7.2.
25. John 10.22.

26. John 7.37–39.
27. Luke 24.26.
28. John 3.14; 8.28; 12.32, 34.
29. John 7.39; 12.16, 23, 28; 13.31f.; 17.1.
30. John 12.28; 13.31; 14.13; 17.1.
31. John 1.29.
32. John 12.27.

Index of Biblical References

Index